"As one of the original viewers, Mr. McMoneagle helped design and build an effective paranormal unit that serviced nearly all major Intelligence Agencies within the Federal Government for seventeen years. After retirement from the Army he was hired by Cognitive Science Lab, which was the laboratory responsible for the research and development of the STARGATE project. He is currently fully employed by them today, doing both research on psychic functionings and RV."

—*Journal of Scientific Exploration*

Also by Joseph McMoneagle

Mind Trek

The Ultimate Time Machine

Remote Viewing Secrets

A HANDBOOK

Joseph McMoneagle

HAMPTON ROADS
PUBLISHING COMPANY, INC.

Cover design by Mayapriya Long
Background cover image by Digital Stock

For information write:
Hampton Roads Publishing Company, Inc.
1125 Stoney Ridge Road
Charlottesville, VA 22902

Or call: 434-296-2772
FAX: 434-296-5096
e-mail: hrpc@hrpub.com
www.hrpub.com

If you are unable to order this book from your local
bookseller, you may order directly from the publisher.
Quantity discounts for organizations are available.
Call 1-800-766-8009, toll-free.

Library of Congress Catalog Card Number: 99-95410

ISBN 1-57174-159-3

10 9 8 7 6

Printed on acid-free paper in the United States

Dedication

This book is dedicated to
my Mom and Dad
because I know they know.

All of reality bows to
the illusion of
Life and Death.

Table of Contents:

Remote Viewing Secrets

A HANDBOOK

Introduction

※

It would be foolish to believe that everything you are going to learn from this book will agree with everything other people say or write about remote viewing. One of the great mysteries of remote viewing is the fact that so many different individuals can perform equally well within its structure. However, having said that, it is also important to know that a few rules do apply and that it is necessary to learn and strictly follow them if you really wish to use remote viewing as it was originally intended.

Not just anything can be called remote viewing. There are students of the paranormal, skeptics, government officials, military, teachers (real and self-proclaimed), and even scientists who think they know something about remote viewing but who, in truth, haven't a clue. I would find myself in one of these groups, were it not for the fact that I have spent a considerable period of my life totally immersed within the research and development side of remote viewing, primarily with the laboratory that started it all, the Cognitive Sciences Lab (CSL).

If I had to pick a single place where remote viewing has been tested, re-tested, and evaluated, or where the many aspects of targeting, analysis, and the methodologies associated with them have been looked at the most, it would have to be CSL. I have spent almost fifteen years there as both research associate and subject, and I am still employed full-time by that organization. In addition, I was one of the original remote viewers recruited into what is now commonly referred to as Project STARGATE, the once secret Army project designed to use trained remote viewers for intelligence purposes during the Cold War. As such, I did applications (sometimes referred to as operational) remote viewing in support of that unit for a period of nearly eighteen years, until it closed in November 1995. Since then, I've continued privately to do applications remote viewing for numerous companies and individuals, and research remote viewing for CSL and other laboratories.

I've seen a lot of water pass under the bridge and developed a unique perspective on teaching and learning remote viewing. Twenty-one years' experience in something as ephemeral as remote viewing may not be something one would normally want to claim, but it is what I do and I do it very well. And, as a result, I know quite a bit about it.

One very large caution needs to be introduced at this point. It would be wrong to imply that I am the only one who knows something about remote viewing. Over the course of eighteen years, counting support and viewer personnel, probably eighty to eighty-five people were involved in the project on both the scientific and the operational sides of the house. For a time, operations were performed by both as were some scientific testing and evaluation. Probably fewer than three dozen people were viewers. Of the others, about half were scientists, and the remainder performed support functions, such as evaluation, analysis, and operational monitoring. It's important to understand that no one individual was ever considered to be more important than any other. It always took a great deal of teamwork and effort to accomplish the mission—scientific, operational, or otherwise.

So, why would there be differences of opinion regarding remote viewing, especially regarding teaching or learning it? Contrary to what one might think, these differences are usually not as great as they may initially appear. To the uninitiated, they may seem to be, but they really aren't. Also, many things that are being stated as fact about remote viewing need to be put into context in order to understand why such differences of opinion occur.

For instance: some members of the unit may say that they believe anyone can be taught remote viewing. Others seem to say something quite the opposite—that remote viewing cannot be taught. In actuality, neither statement is quite true within such a narrow context. This is one of the unfortunate results of living in an age where the single line statement or "sound bite" is important. It is usually all you get. It is not surprising that given the above two sound bites, one would assume that two different things are being said and that there is a great chasm of difference between them. In writing this handbook, I hope to clarify for the reader where real difference lies and where it doesn't. I want everyone to understand that most of us really are in agreement and the diversity of opinion is not only healthy but a requirement if we are to progress in any growth of understanding of remote viewing.

A Short History

It is not my intention to re-write the history of remote viewing. What I will do, however, is to tell people where they can get it. If you are interested in one person's viewpoint about the early days of remote viewing and his own role within it, then you will have to gain access to the Internet World Wide Web. Once you have, then log onto Mr. Ingo Swann's web site at: <u>www.biomindsuperpowers.com/Pages/RealStoryMain.html</u>.

He has written one of the most detailed and lengthy early histories available on the subject. Everything he says on that site is probably about as accurate as one can be with personal perceptions, at least from a historical viewpoint. However, you should remember that it is also a singular and one-sided view of those events, and that it contains very little data relating to the classified military project. Arguments will almost certainly arise about those years from others who were there at the time and perhaps saw things somewhat differently. One should remember, however, that disagreements should not affect how one thinks about the veracity of remote viewing itself.

Also, in commenting on the history of remote viewing, it would be unethical not to refer to a little known writing by a man named René Warcollier. He wrote a book titled *Mind To Mind*, which was published by Creative Age Press of New York in 1948. It was originally conceived as a lecture that he delivered at the Sorbonne in June 1946, under the title, "A Contribution to the Study of Mental Imagery Through Telepathic Drawing." This lecture was essentially a report on hundreds of what he called telepathic experiments that he had carried out over a period of nearly forty years. His approach, attempts at control, unique deference to drawings, and the statistical results in his experiments are very applicable to remote viewing research going on today. Those truly interested in pursuing remote viewing as something more than a hobby should try to obtain a copy of this book before beginning.

That the Cognitive Science Laboratory at SRI-International put Remote Viewing on the map cannot be disputed. CSL received a considerable amount of funding, carried out and supported extensive experimentation, and provided support to intelligence operations from 1972 through 1995. If this had not occurred, then no Project STARGATE would have existed, and remote-viewing history would have been very short indeed. A little-known fact about CSL that needs to be said here is that the money spent on experimentation during the 23-year period was not all spent there. It was shared through numerous sub-contracts with many other labs, enabling a great deal of research into the paranormal to be accomplished in areas sometimes only peripherally related to remote viewing. This led to greater understanding of everything from methods of evaluation, to establishing statistical standards, to how a human brain might be appropriately studied.

These accomplishments were and are directly attributable to Dr. Hal Puthoff and Mr. Russell Targ in the early years, 1972 through 1986—and to Dr. Edwin C. May and his colleagues—from 1986 through the termination of the project in November 1995. (I need to add that Dr. May worked for approximately nine plus years at CSL prior to becoming its director in 1986.)

In addition, dozens of other scientists worked at CSL between 1972 and 1995, some of whom have become leaders in various fields, as well as directors of other labs or organizations on the cutting edge of investigations into the nature of humankind. I am underscoring this fact so that the reader understands there was no dearth of real and solid science within the history or background of remote viewing. This science should rightfully carry a great deal of weight when readers decide what they should or shouldn't do or believe about remote viewing and its appropriate form or application.

I should also state here that findings and materials from the lab were shared and used within the operational element of Project STARGATE, located at Fort Meade, Maryland, at least for most of the time it existed. As a result of managerial difficulties, there were periods during which this did not happen. This is the basis for at least three significant areas of disagreement that might arise among past members of that unit.

These are:

a. Research that established changes to specific remote viewing applications was sometimes not viewed as constructive or conducive to the operational requirements by the Fort Meade project managers. In such cases, this research was summarily dismissed as unnecessary or simply discarded. Since these suggestions were almost always implemented at CSL but not at the Meade Unit, there is not only disagreement over their necessity, but a total lack of understanding about their efficacy or the research necessitating the original or recommended changes.

b. There was always a large discrepancy between good managers and bad managers within STAR-GATE. Some took the time and trouble to learn about and completely understand both the operational and the scientific minimums and maximums. (In other words, there were things that remote viewing should and should not be used for.) This means that for eighteen years, there were numerous periods of appropriate and inappropriate tasking, the application of various appropriate and inappropriate methodologies, and a multitude of evaluation techniques that may or may not have been appropriate at any given time. Since full managerial responsibility for the project resided within the Meade unit, the science side of the house was sometimes subjected to these irregularities, as were certainly the remote viewers. At times, this had a major impact on both the project overall, and the people within it.

c. When you deal with the paranormal, you deal with a unique field that has a tendency to polarize individuals at one extreme or the other—from the hardened non-believer (narrow-minded debunker-type personality) to the zealot (who will believe almost anything). The people in the military are not divinely inspired, so they are no exception to this. The military had and has its fair share of very polarized individuals, some more so than others. Some were inside and others were outside the STARGATE Unit.

So, one can easily understand the vast lines of difference that may be at issue and which are generally responsible for the large degree of disagreement that seems to exist among individuals within the field. Having worked for both the operational and the scientific sides of the house, I must argue that when in doubt, one should nearly always give sway to the scientific version of why things happen or don't happen.

The simple reason for this is that if you attempt to defend remote viewing (which, remember, is a paranormal function) from strictly an operational viewpoint, you will almost assuredly lose the battle. This is particularly true when trying to defend remote viewing against a healthy and skeptical viewpoint. While applications of remote viewing may present some very nice anecdotal examples of success, they leave too many explanations for why they might have happened other than remote viewing. The battles are tough enough when the facts are backed by science, even science performed under the strict guidelines of numerous scientific over-sight committees. This is one of the primary reasons CSL always functioned with at least three of these committees between 1986 and 1995.

Those wishing to pursue a more detailed history of the Cognitive Sciences Laboratory and what it has to say about remote viewing can do so on the Internet at: www.lfr.org/csl/index.html.

Since this is a handbook on remote viewing, there is no

reason to go into any greater detail regarding its history. I am sure that many individuals will make this attempt in the future. I only ask that when considering this history, remember that probably better than ninety-nine percent of the hard material required to establish that history resides within three areas:

a. The people who were participants in STARGATE, each having a uniquely different view, and each possessing knowledge for a finite period of time within the unit.

b. The Operational, or Fort Meade Unit, for which ninety-nine percent of the material has not yet been declassified or made available to the public.

c. The Cognitive Sciences Laboratory, where arguably the majority of actual research took place. A significant portion of this material has already been published in peer review journals[1] and within refereed papers. However, like the operational material, quite a bit of this material remains classified.

Teaching and Learning

So, does this mean that anyone can learn to remote view and everyone can learn to do it equally well?

The answer is actually yes and no.

As a result of the research and the applications, there are many things we now understand about remote viewing that we didn't know at the beginning. We know that how one approaches the target, how the remote viewer is managed, or how the information is handled will have decisive effects on the results. We know a lot more about the appropriate versus inappropriate way that remote

---

[1] A list of these publications can be found in Appendix F.

viewing should be applied and how not to oversell it. We know about destructive versus constructive remote viewer habits while receiving information, processing it, and translating it to paper or tape. We probably know as much about what shouldn't be done as what should be done during a remote viewing. We know details regarding the correct protocols, specifics about differing methodologies, exceptions that exist between training and applications, unique forms of employment, good and bad practices, how to leverage information with time, efficient and dysfunctional front-loading, and dozens of other inside tracks to the very heart of effective remote viewing. We understand to some degree the probable consequences of diet, or the reverse, how remote viewing might affect one's health. All of these things can be taught, learned, and applied.

Can everyone be taught to do equally as well as the next person in remote viewing? No. No more than you can successfully teach everyone to be top of the line competitors in swimming, track, shooting, or golf.

Experience dictates that it's probably a mixture of desire and focus (33%), quality and intensity of training (33%), and the natural talent you walk in the door with (33%). How do you know if you have what it takes? Well, that's what this book is all about.

Chapter One

— ✳ —

The Martial Art
of Remote Viewing

Michel Random states in the preface to his book, *The Martial Arts, Swordsmanship, Kendo, Aikido, Judo, Karate;* Octopus Books Limited, 1977:

Modern myths about superman, the invincible wrecker, constitute a dangerous temptation to stretch the energy bow to the point at which the string snaps, where the being literally explodes within. Even if such beings become commercial idols, objects of public acclaim, they are nevertheless still inarticulate puppets brought to life with artificial power and energy, who inevitably turn on each other because they have not been assimilated in real terms. Energy is what one makes of it. It can be a source of life or a source of death, a creation or destruction. There is no wisdom exclusive to budo and budo does not escape universal wisdom in which finality is neither retraction nor the drying up of the intellect but its totality and harmony. To be in this sense means to know, and to know is to add energy to energy, life to life, love to love. Such is the way of the universe.

When he wrote these words, he was addressing budo, or Way of the Warrior, in a martial art sense. However, having studied the martial arts as well as remote viewing for over twenty years, I have to say that remote viewing, at least as I have come to understand it, can be expressed in the very same manner.

Remote viewing is a way—*RV'do*[2]. It's a discipline, a science, and a technique containing certain principles that cannot, and should not, be diluted. As in the martial arts, the methods or *styles* that have come into play may be different, but the essential principles that underscore the foundations for its practice should not and cannot be changed.

These principles dictate that to be taught and taught well, one must not only learn those aspects that can be practiced through repetition under protocol, but also the more ephemeral realities which impact directly the fundamental rules of integrity that bind it all together. Practice is the *mind's body* being conditioned, and the philosophy or spirituality that supports this conditioning is the *mind's soul*.

The Right State of Mind

We like to think of all Japanese martial arts masters as being Zen Buddhists, but they are not. The traditional and original religion of Japan is Shinto. Shinto literally means "the way of kami," and kami means "mystical." Shinto has no founder, no official scriptures or texts, and no dogma, and even thus unencumbered has survived the ages, to include the coming of Buddhism in the year 538. As a result of varying changes to Buddhism, Zen was introduced to Japan sometime during the thirteenth century. Zen cannot be described very well other than by saying what it is "not." It is not a system of ideas, metaphysics, or religion. It is even less endowed with dogma, belief, vows, or symbols than the rest.

---

[2] *RV'do* is a registered trademark.

Within Zen one seeks nothing. You can gain no merit, no faith is required of you, no savior is necessary, there is no just reward, no choice in all things, nor is there any desire for attainment.

When I am asked about what one must learn in order to do remote viewing, my normal response is: "Zen." Zen meditation brings a strong emphasis on the mental and spiritual state of the practitioner. The rationalizing and calculating functions of the mind are suspended so that the mind and body can react immediately and in unison to an outside influence. In martial arts, this could be a physical threat. To the remote viewer, it is the completion of a thought without thought being necessary.[3]

In following the way of remote viewing, one learns to be an empty vessel, within which ideas can form that are relevant to an unknown location, event, object, person, or concept. These ideas are not connected to any personal desires, wants, issues, beliefs, or structures that may already exist within us.

Since there is no way of really describing the perfect experience of such intimate and thorough knowledge as occurs during the sharing of subject and target, training becomes more of an *unlearning* of habits developed since childhood. These are habits that get in the way of that perfect symbiosis between mind and target.

The right state of mind during remote viewing is very much like attempting to mentally balance on a fine wire fence. In making an effort to find that perfect point of balance within the void, you reach a point of exclusion of all other thought. It's only the sudden realization that you are in harmony, perfectly balanced on the edge, which ruins the state of being. As explained by many Zen Masters, it is a condition of mind that is nearly as difficult to master as it is to describe.

---

[3] A list of these publications can be found in Appendix F.

Therefore, a right state of mind is essential to the pursuing of RV'do. Developing this right state of mind requires the following, at a minimum:

a. Elimination of the negative aspects of ego. When it comes to remote viewing expertise, following a doctrine of individual self-interest is highly corrosive to your ultimate goals. An exaggerated sense of self-importance will always be destructive to the higher goal. Self-importance requires that you set escalating levels of excellence. You quickly find that the expectations are impossible to fulfill. Fear of failure becomes your master.

b. Complete relinquishment of any personal expectation for perfection. You will probably never find perfection in remote viewing. It is just like any of your other senses. Mistakes will be made, filters will sometimes be turned on or off inappropriately, or your perceptive apertures will not be exacting enough. Setting specific or personalized expectations will only complicate matters. It will make it more difficult for you to deal with failure when it occurs, and will increase the number of those failures. You need to understand from the outset that each of us learns in our own way, we learn at our own speed, and success is measured differently for each of us. There is no way to compare yourself against those who have come before you. Nor is it necessary to do so.

c. Both spiritual as well as philosophic growth will be required. Remote viewing is compatible with strong faith in a higher order, a greater being or energy, and should not be in any way offensive to your religious beliefs.

d. The word fear in all of its permutations will have to be eliminated from your vocabulary. Fear breeds paranoia, anger, and resentment, and is thoroughly destructive to the remote viewing process. Fear implies a tacit agreement to participate in the root or negative energies that lie at the very basis of its own creation. If you think that you will be harmed, then you will be, and if you think that something is evil then it is. We are our own worst enemies when it comes to the generation of fear and the dark side.

e. Finally, a continued and balanced pursuit of the truth will be required. You must, above all else, sustain your ability to think critically, to ask questions, to maintain a healthy skepticism, and to walk the centerline of acceptable reality. Acceptable reality in this case being a mid-point, somewhere between either perceived extreme. The ease with which one is capable of deluding oneself in this field is legendary. The distance between knowing something to be true, and believing it, can be measured in less than the blink of an eye. One's credibility is as fragile as a powder-blue bird's egg. Once cracked, it is shattered irreparably and forevermore lies somewhere just beyond reach, one more body bag of bones on some media heap.

In building a new house, a lot of attention is paid to the foundation. Great care is focused on the steel reinforced concrete footer upon which the rest of the house will sit. Long before it begins to even look like a house, the solid stone walls, core filled cinder blocks, or formed concrete walls are constructed and then buried beneath tons of earth fill. Even though much of this construction will never be seen again, it is the care and meticulous attention to detail in building the foundation that dictates the longevity, strength, and support inherent within the finished structure.

The above spoke to this foundation, now comes the upper structure.

Chapter Two

—— ✳ ——

Levels of Remote Viewing

I'm not actually sure that specific levels of remote viewing can be established. There has been some attempt by others to do this, but the difficulty lies in the fact that all of us mentally process information differently. As long as we do, no two people can ever be expected to react the same while developing their remote viewing capability. In fact, you should expect to see differences between individuals from the very beginning of their exposure.

However, by nature, we think in levels and somewhat expect them. So as a guide, I will show what the average person can expect. In keeping with the concept of RV'do, I've laid these out much like the different belts one might expect to find within a martial art. I will attempt to describe each of these as completely as possible.

White Belt

This will usually be the beginner or novitiate, someone being exposed to remote viewing for the first time. There is great honor in being called a novitiate. For every *Omega*, or ending, there has to be an *Alpha*, a beginning. Everyone who truly understands the martial arts understands that the beginning is right where we hope to eventually arrive.

All masters begin with a white belt and a first introduction to technique. Years later, when they have sufficiently mastered not just one technique, but many, they are able to synthesize what they have learned into something both powerful and simple. The key to becoming a master is to take what is necessary from others, use it to identify your own natural talent or skill, and then create something equally effective, but it is hoped with a much greater simplicity and grace.

So, the beginning remote viewer can expect to learn a very basic or initial technique at this stage. It should be simple enough to grasp, powerful enough to produce a basic level of response, but significant enough to show there is more (with effort) available.

The viewer with a white belt can expect to describe a major gestalt, but very little else. A gestalt is the sum of the elements that create an overall impression of a target. Much of the information that a white belt can expect to see will be fractured almost beyond recognition and will have very few inter-connections. In other words, a lot of it won't make any sense at all.

Besides the active remote viewing itself, white belt viewers should come to understand some of the rules. For instance, they should learn the differences between good protocols and bad protocols. They should be able to define what remote viewing is, and the differences between remote viewing and other forms of paranormal behavior. (Most of this can be found in Chapter Three.)

Following is an example of a target with a remote viewing result that can be expected from a white belt viewer:

Actual target   **Expected result**

Yellow Belt

The differences between white and yellow are probably not going to seem very significant, but they are. This is when viewers begin to receive more input that is recognizable as delivered from their "senses." In fact, this is a term that is commonly used; "I *sense* there is a lot of red at the target site."

This skill level usually results in the first use of the word "like" as well. "It's. . . .well. . . .*like* a swimming pool, but not actually a swimming pool."

The reason for this change is because you have essentially discovered the place in your mind where the data arrives, but you have absolutely no control over how much processing you do with it. In fact, you still have no control over fully accessing it.

Overall or general descriptions of the targets can be expected, as well as a very general feel for the environment.

Besides the actual remote viewing, yellow belt students should begin to learn about the necessary mental requirements, competency, stability, intelligence, and educational requirements. They should understand the negative aspects of remote viewing and what effects can be expected from mental instability. They should be taught how their experiences will affect those around them, such as family, friends, or acquaintances. (Much of this will be presented within Chapter Four.) The following is an example of a yellow belt viewer's results:

Actual target

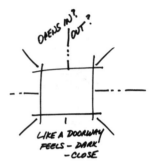

Expected result

Orange Belt

This level of learning can be summed up in the words, *aesthetic impact*. Aesthetic impact deals with how the remote viewer's sense of art, beauty, and taste are affected.

Things you most like and dislike about the target will become evident. The problem with this is that it will also become difficult to tell where the actual target information begins or ends, and where your imagination lies in relationship to it. The orange belt viewer will have a lot of difficulty in getting a handle on the natural creative process and separating it from the actual target information source.

The upside is that previously confusing details will begin to come together in meaningful ways that show links and connections within the target. At the same time, you will begin to recognize or notice internally generated overlay. We call this "analytic overlay", because it is generally produced in the processing portion of the mind and has nothing to do with the actual remote viewing data as delivered in its raw form.

While this is one of the more demanding stages of remote viewing learning, it can also be one of the fun stages. If you pay attention, you will learn a lot about how and why you process information the way you do, and you will be able to unhook from many of the bad habits you've picked up along the way in your human development.

A small example would be: A *sense* of bright, reflected-light from a surface, for most people, almost automatically means there is glass in the target. However, over time, one learns that the *sense* of bright, reflected light can also come from concrete, steel or metal, a large area of white sand, the surface of water, a mirror, windows, or can be artificially produced. So we quickly learn about a bad habit called, *assumption*.

Besides the viewing aspects of this stage, orange belt viewers should also learn about how viewers are selected, how some develop more talent than others and why. This will enable them to overcome the key issues in themselves that might be preventing them from becoming better viewers.

This stage is what I call the first of three "make or break" stages. This is where aspiring new viewers find out whether or not they have what it takes to continue on in a learning process that really has no end. Whether they want to devote a significant portion of their life to understanding and becoming centered in "RV'do." (Much of this information can be found in Chapter Five.) Following is an example of yellow belt viewing:

Actual target   **Expected result**

Brown Belt

Emotions begin to hammer in. You will find as you enter the brown belt stage that you have to learn to deal with emotions. These will be emotions that are generated within the target, as well as your emotional reaction to what might be perceived about the target. This doesn't sound like much, but it is one of the most difficult things a remote viewer has to overcome.

Emotions are primal reactions to events and circumstances that we have developed within us over a long period of time. We generally react emotionally to things long before we are able to think about them in a rational sense. So, emotions cloud the viewing material, they make it more difficult to define the details, and overlay it with preconceived thoughts.

Since this is also where we begin to form conclusions, it creates a very dangerous combination. Most have enough experience to know that what you *think* you are "seeing" is sometimes not what you *feel* you are seeing.

I'm reminded of a scene in a movie where Mel Gibson sees his partner's daughter being assaulted. He reacts emotionally to the situation, jumping the perpetrator from behind, and pummeling him to the ground. Unfortunately, it turns out that she has gotten a job as an actress and they are in the middle of filming a scene on a street set.

At this stage of viewing it is very easy to make this kind of mistake: leaping to a conclusion. It is also quite easy to get wrapped up in the emotion of another person at the target and to imagine what they might be feeling, based on the details. These kinds of emotions may or may not be correct.

What is good about this stage of learning is that it forces us to slow down, to pay very close attention to the details. We come to realize over time there are a number of conclusions that might fit a given like or similar collection of details.

For example: A large square filled with water might not be a swimming pool. It could be a septic tank, a fishpond without fish, a reflecting pool, or a holding tank. A tall thin object with what seems like fronds at the top could be a palm tree or it might also be a television antenna.

If one pays attention at this stage, a lot can be learned about how you should be putting the details together.

Viewers working on their brown belt in RV'do should also be learning all about the various methods or techniques that can be used in remote viewing. They should be garnering a clear understanding of the pros and cons regarding the types of targets, why some targets make very good remote viewing targets, and why some don't.

Strange and unique protocols have been developed over the years to address very narrow or specific kinds of remote viewing targets, such as: binary questions (yes/no, right/wrong, buy/don't buy, etc.), healing, sub-atomic or microtargeting, event-related problems, etc. These should all be clearly understood by this point.

Some rather exotic forms, methods, or techniques can be learned as well. The brown belt viewer should have at least a firm knowledge of what these are, and the pros and cons regarding each. (Information on these subjects can be found in Chapter Six.) An example of brown belt viewing follows:

Actual target

Expected result

Black Belt (First Stage)

Entering this belt region, one begins to refine ideas and concepts pertinent to the target. These are concepts that drive the target situation. Why things are happening the way they are and what the eventual outcome should be.

This is the level of remote viewing that permits drawing to scale, correctly proportioning elements in the target to each other, and the interconnection between one target area and another. It is where the viewer begins to understand the full relationship of people within the target, their motivations, and why they are there. This skill level represents interrelationships of elements within the target, gives the target meaning.

Analysis of target material will be very good at this stage, but not yet perfect. One can expect to be hitting a randomly chosen target at least fifty percent of the time, and one should be able to produce 30 to 50 percent information that makes a lot of sense about the target, shows significant details, and/or establishes solid conclusions about the target.

At this point, besides viewing techniques, the new black belt viewer should have a very clear understanding of the learning and teaching methods they have been subjected to. They should understand what can be imparted by a teaching method and what cannot be, or what is dependent on talent. They should be learning the details surrounding the application of remote viewing—why there are differences between the learning methods and the methods of application.

By the time Black Belts (First Stage) finish their training, they should be able to identify and select appropriate targets for learning, and be able to properly set up a target for applications purposes. (Selection of appropriate targets is presented in Chapter Seven.) The results of a Black Belt (First Stage) viewing follow:

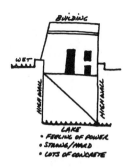

Actual target   **Expected result**

Black Belt (Second Stage)

The entire structure of remote viewing should change at this point. Typically, viewers will no longer be thinking about targets the way they have up until now.

Drawings will become three-dimensional and the hidden aspects of a target will begin to shine through. Viewers will have a very clear perception of where they are in relation to the target and will be able to shift that perception at will.

This is a very hard stage to maintain and it cannot easily be done by even the most proficient of viewers. This is the second "make or break" level of viewing. The majority of those who learn to remote view and who devote a considerable amount of time and effort to doing so usually bottom out at this point. This more than likely has to do with philosophical belief structure; that is, it depends on what they can change within themselves and what they cannot.

Most of what we can see and understand about our beliefs we can usually change. But, there are a lot of things, philosophically, that we are never able to see. Just because someone is exposed to the possibilities, does not guarantee they will observe or become cognizant of them.

There are aspects about time/space that will always remain just beyond the reach of some individuals. No matter how hard they try, they will never see or understand the next layer.

From a practical standpoint, there is nothing wrong with that. In fact, attempting to force change in someone at this level can result in severe damage to the psyche. This area sits along the edge of reason. Forcing the issue here is not recommended.

However, a second stage black belt can still learn the non-viewing aspects of this stage, which deal with "front loading." Up until this point, I have not addressed this very critical issue, because learning anything about it without understanding the basis for all of the stages that come before would only create confusion and misunderstanding. (This is covered in quite a lot of detail in Chapter Eight.) An example of this viewing level is presented as follows:

Actual target

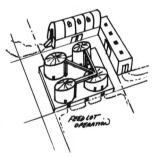

Expected result

Black Belt (Third Stage)

Third stage black belts should be able to lay out the target's entire history within the context of abstract expression, and should be able to detail the target's connections or place in reality and space/time.

This really opens the door on history and the future and how the target flows through time. This is also about the best that anyone can be expected to do with regard to remote viewing ability. The skills that follow are much more advanced, and while not absolutely necessary to the remote viewing process as it is used in day-to-day applications, they can bring a much deeper understanding of RV'do to the practitioner.

Someone who reaches this level and who can display such ability on a consistent basis can meet any challenge. There are no remote viewing targets or conditions they should not be able to address.

It would be appropriate to state that someone who has reached this stage is, or should be considered, a Master of RV'do. There is no necessity to go beyond this point. However, some will want to.

In a non-viewing sense, this level is where one learns all about time, what is probably real about it, and what is probably not real. Targeting the past, present, and future all require unique conditions that someone at this level must clearly understand. (Information regarding these forms of targeting can be found in Chapter Nine.)

Additional skills that should be mastered at this level are: reporting, formal record keeping, unique/strange features known to impact on remote viewing, and other paranormal disciplines impacting on/supporting remote viewing. (These are found in Chapters Ten and Eleven.)

An example of this viewing level demonstrates the increase in depth and knowledge about the target. In many cases, a viewer will present near perfect drawings of the target.

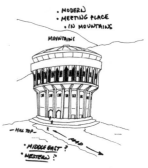

Actual target   **Expected results**

Place of Worship.
Place where people of like culture congregate.
Large and very open inside.
Middle Eastern.
Modern building reflecting ancient architecture.

Black Belt (Fourth Stage)

This is the third "make or break" point. This is where the Master is introduced into a different type or level of knowledge.

Manifestations and apparitions in and outside the specified target begin to occasionally occur. This is where wisdom becomes a real aspect of the structure. I'm not talking about wisdom as in knowledge we can be taught, I'm talking about wisdom that is imparted about the human condition. This form of wisdom has nothing to do with "local" definitions of right or wrong; but has everything to do with human dignity and righteousness, how human beings should be respected and/or treated.

The Master of RV'do at this level begins to see elements of reality that usually remain hidden, having to do with constructive and destructive ideals; ideals that lay buried beneath or behind the nature of things. Spontaneous knowing and understanding is automatic at this stage. Knowing when it is a correct *knowing* versus a false *belief* is also learned at this time. A full understanding of reality's intricate interactions becomes apparent. Also, one obtains at least a partial understanding of how to alter future outcomes through action, as well as the healing of self and others. Some of these aspects are lightly touched upon in Chapter Thirteen. Most of these conditions are not being experienced full time nor are they very well controlled by the individual when the occur.

Red/Black Belt—Great Master

What takes place here is a full integration of everything learned with what is now understood about one's own strengths and weaknesses. It is a place of self-realization, a time of intense spiritual and ethical cleansing. It is where the student of RV'do evolves back to the *Alpha* point, the beginning.

It is the ultimate position of focus and understanding. But it is also a position of greatest simplicity. It is a near-perfect union of one's paranormal talent blended within extant reality. People who reach this level no longer have to think about how to do it, they simply do.

Chapter Three

— ✳ —

What Remote Viewing Is

What defines remote viewing is sometimes difficult for the layman or beginning remote viewer to understand. In fact, at times things can become so complex that a scientist would have difficulty ensuring that remote viewing and not something else is actually taking place, because remote viewing is so similar to other things like psychic functioning. Psychics function in myriad ways. Some do what is called a "cold reading," where they sit in front of someone and describe things that are going on in their lives. While this takes a great deal of sensitivity to other people, it does not necessarily guarantee that an actual transfer of information is taking place in a psychic way.

We know, for instance, that just being in the room with someone who knows the answer to something and being allowed to study them for a short period of time is sometimes sufficient to obtain information they possess without ever addressing it directly. They don't have to pass it to us verbally and they don't have to write it down. Through observation alone, they will eventually generate sufficient information to tell us what we need to know.

People do this in a lot of different ways. Remember when you were a child and you played that game where you would hide something and then give hints to someone looking for it, as they moved around a room, "You're getting warmer, you're getting warmer, you're hot, uh-oh you're on fire!"

Well, I'm talking about the same kind of thing. For instance, the way a person shifts in a chair might tell us when we are getting close to a correct answer. How people fold their arms during a conversation or what they do with their hands transfer information as well. Even where and how a person moves his eyes while answering a question can tell us whether we are right or wrong, or if they are inventing a response to throw us off the track, or if they simply don't know.

Psychics who sometimes use different tools in order to practice their trade further complicate these situations. They might be scrying from a crystal ball or interpreting the cards in a Tarot deck. Some psychics get their information spontaneously, in a natural or untrained way. My point is that most psychics generally operate within the boundaries of their own rules. They do not follow specifically developed or designed and tested remote viewing protocols. Being a remote viewer requires a lot more than is required of a psychic.

This doesn't mean that psychics operating on their own are less capable than remote viewers; it just means their techniques are different, and different techniques or methods operating *outside of an appropriate protocol*, do have a direct affect on whether or not someone is actually remote viewing.

Therefore: remote viewing is the ability to produce information that is correct about a place, event, person, object, or concept which is located somewhere else in time/space, and which is completely blind to the remote viewer and others taking part in the process of collecting the information.

Two other requirements are:

   a. All persons present during a remote viewing should essentially be blind to the target.

This is almost always true, except for very specific or very restricted forms of targeting material that can sometimes be used. This type of targeting material is addressed later on within this handbook. By necessity, these more complex methods of targeting and the materials required are only used by those who clearly understand how, where, why, and when they should be used.

b. There should be some form or means of validating the material after the remote viewing has been accomplished.

In other words, there should be feedback of some kind. There should also be some way of checking it for accuracy, or validating that the information is correct.

These requirements certainly set remote viewing apart from other forms of paranormal information collection, and there is a reason for this. Currently about sixty people, and eight or nine laboratories, have spent more than twenty-five years of work, sweat, thought, and a considerable amount of money, establishing the veracity of remote viewing through very extensive study. During this time, these people were very clear in defining the ground rules and protocols that were necessary in order to call it remote viewing. They did not do this just to separate remote viewing from other forms of the paranormal. They did it so that remote viewing would *not* be viewed like any other form of paranormal functioning. They did it so that their new research techniques could bring some validity and credibility to the study of paranormal functioning vis-à-vis remote viewing. And, to a certain extent they did it just to be different.

Those who throw something together and call it remote viewing do a disservice to these people, these labs, and dilute the very value and significance that these studies have brought to the paranormal field. They also dilute the entire concept of looking at remote viewing as a martial art—RV'do.

Definitions

The primary differences between the words *protocol* and *method* lie within the word origins and the specific circumstances in which they are usually used. Since understanding these differences are fundamental to understanding the rest of this book, I present them here:

A Protocol

A remote viewing protocol is a detailed plan of a scientific experiment, treatment, or procedure. It is the first step and a necessary one in the design of an application.

Since it is scientific, it is usually designed and tested within a lab, usually through consensus of researchers. Once tested, it is open to review, evaluation, and publication in an already established and respected forum to determine its validity. As a result it may be changed a number of times before it becomes acceptable to the majority who pass judgment on it. It is then often tested again at other labs with other subjects and replicated before it is used in an application format. Designing and testing a protocol is necessary in order to validate the technique or method subsequently designed from or based upon it.

In remote viewing, a protocol can have many different methods or techniques based on it, but the protocol itself is never altered.

Method or Technique

A method or technique is a systematic procedure or mode of inquiry employed by or proper to a particular discipline or art. In remote viewing, these are always applied within the framework of a protocol.

This primarily has to do with consistency of form. A method is how you decide to approach a problem to produce a solution. In most cases, it is designed to be repetitive and it can in some cases be used to teach or learn a skill. It determines structure through which you progress to an end result. It does not have to be particularly scientific or approved by anyone except the person who designs it or decides to use it. The reason for using a specific method is to accomplish a task or to impart specific knowledge from one individual to another. In remote viewing, using a method without concern for protocol can quickly lead to exaggerated, artificial, or misleading results.

For example: Ignoring the requirement that a monitor also be blind to a target and inappropriately front loading that individual with too much knowledge about the target will inevitably result in the possibility of inappropriate actions or statements occurring inside the room during the remote viewing. These create a possibility that the remote viewer will be led to certain conclusions, invalidating the rest of the process.

While some people claim they can control this, experience and studies suggest otherwise. The smallest possibility that such an action will result in a "cooked" result is sufficient to damage the reputation of remote viewing, and it most certainly taints the results.

Application

A remote viewing application is the production of information through the use of a technique or method based on a tested protocol.

All techniques and methods used in remote viewing should be based on or designed around properly tested and validated protocols. The reason for such a strict measure is to guarantee that what is thought to be happening actually is. It is to insure that those participating in collecting the information are not deluding themselves into thinking something is happening that isn't.

Differences in Protocols

There are sometimes differences in protocols. The following are examples of some of the different protocols that have been used in the past. These are addressed in more detail in the appendix of this book:

1. Outbounder Remote Viewing. Requires a person to act as a beacon and to be present at the targeted site or event.

2. Associative Remote Viewing. Uses proxy targets to obtain binary (e.g., yes/no/other) responses.

3. Coordinate Remote Viewing. Uses numeric or Alpha/numeric series to identify the specific target.

4. Precognitive Remote Viewing. Provides information that is predictive in nature, or provides information on a target before it has been selected.

Differences in Methods

Methods of remote viewing are the forms or styles of viewing which remote viewers choose to use while remote viewing. In some cases these are used within a remote viewing protocol, but in some cases they are not. When they are, it is remote viewing; when they are not, then it is not remote viewing.

Examples for some of these are: ERV (Extended Remote Viewing), CRV (first known as Coordinate Remote Viewing, now known as Controlled Remote Viewing), SRV (Scientific Remote Viewing) that is scientific in name only, and TRV (Technical Remote Viewing)[4] a variation on CRV.

There are others, but this gives an idea how remote viewing methodologies have evolved, either for better or worse. Some of these are used within approved protocols,

---

[4] Scientific Remote Viewing (SRV), and Technical Remote Viewing (TRV) are registered trademarks.

some are not, and some have been used both ways because people using them did not or do not understand the basic differences between protocols and the methods they are wedded to. Many of these were used within Project STARGATE but some were not.

This training handbook is not designed to provide detailed explanations for all of the methods currently being used, or to validate them in any way. It is designed to help you understand the differences between a method that is being used properly and one that isn't. By the end of this book you should have a clear idea of which is which.

What Remote Viewing is Best Used For

Remote viewing always operates best when it is used for producing information on something that is known to exist. In other words, one should be assured that the target is real.

Elements of the target should be relatively easy to verify. There is a very good reason for this. For instance, if you are trying to determine the best location in which to proceed with an archeological dig, you should know enough about the surroundings of the dig to ascertain whether or not the remote viewer is generally in the right area to begin with. You should be able to do this without giving too much information to the viewer.

As an example: perhaps you want to do an excavation of an old grave complex, and it's located adjacent to some ruins. This would make an ideal remote viewing target.

Because it is located next to ruins, it permits considerable leeway in the kind of targeting material you can provide to the remote viewer.

In this case, the remote viewer can be asked directly to: "Describe the most important object I am (should be) interested in and draw a ground plan for the best place for me to dig in order to find it."

By keeping the viewer blind to the entire target, you can compare his ground plan to the real thing. If s/he says the most important thing you should be looking for is a mummy wrapped in gold ornaments and located at a specific spot, and you see "ruins" in their drawing, there is a very good chance s/he is on the right target. This makes the rest of what is said more likely to be true as well.

In other words, if what is known matches, then there is a better than even chance that the location and the mummy are probably real as well. If there are no similarities, something isn't working. Try again later using a different targeting approach.

If you had provided the remote viewer knowledge of the ruins in the first place, you would have given up knowledge about the target which might have provided verification on the veracity of the remote viewing. It could also have steered the viewer to a specific time period, based on knowledge of the area in which the dig is taking place. At the very least, this will cloud the target issues with assumptions the viewer may or may not be able to work through.

When you know absolutely nothing about a target in the beginning, it puts everybody in the dark and makes it nearly impossible to evaluate the quality of the remote viewing before you use the product. This is why UFOs and similar kinds of targets usually make lousy remote viewing targets.

What should be understood here is that the remote viewer is always given the least amount of information necessary to put them on the target location, and it should never be directly pertinent to what you are looking for answers to. In most cases, this is simply an envelope or perhaps a photograph of someone who is actually there.

Unknown targets are filled with problems. As an example, a totally unknown target, like a UFO sighting, makes a very poor target. Even if you have a perfect description of the area in which the sighting has taken place, you are still left without any information that can validate specifics about the actual target—the UFOs. In my experience, the chances of stating UFO material obtained through remote viewing is correct are very close to zero.

Likewise, the existence of a totally unknown target is almost never checked out on the ground. In other words, almost no one ever expends the energy or money necessary to determine ground truth about the targeted area.

Another problem is there is almost never any feedback that can be provided to the remote viewer. This does nothing in assisting them to improve their product, or their remote viewing capability.

Therefore, I would say that remote viewing is very good for:

1. DESCRIBING PEOPLE, EVENTS, THINGS, CONCEPTS, PLACES, ETC., WHICH ARE REAL.

It is very good when a partial description is already available or where someone is willing to actually go to the target site to validate or collect material. This means targets should exist in real time and space, should be things you can hold in your hands, or experience, or visit, or in someway establish or verify. You don't have to be able to do that right away, but you should be able to produce some verifiable data within a reasonable period of time. And at some point the viewer should be given hard and factual feedback.

2. PRODUCING NEW LEADS.

This involves assisting in targeting other technologies. No one should be expected to trust remote viewing as a stand-alone source of information, but you should be able to use remote viewing information to align, target, point, or use other technologies. We have equipment that can locate three specific microns amongst trillions, or iron ore from a hundred miles away. Remote viewing is good for pointing this equipment in the right direction. This saves time and in some cases quite a bit of money.

3. RECONSTRUCTING EVENTS.

Remote viewing is very good at filling in the details for events. Very few of us have a memory at our disposal that retains the kinds of detail we would like to have about an event. Where a lot of information has been collected relevant to an event (say a crime), remote viewing is very good at gluing it all together, putting it into a cohesive and understandable pattern, or pointing out the missing pieces.

4. MAKING DECISIONS.

There are unique targeting mechanisms that can be used to aid or assist in decision-making. This is especially true regarding binary problems, e.g., yes or no, go or don't go, buy or don't buy, left or right, up or down, etc.

5. MAKING PROJECTIONS.

When used within a very strict protocol, remote viewing can produce some amazing detail about things that have not yet happened, as long as they are descriptive. However, great caution has to be exercised when it comes to timing. Timing, or projecting when something is going to happen or happened, is something remote viewing is generally not very good at.

Remote Viewing Cannot be Relied upon To:

While remote viewing can be relied upon for many things, there are a number of things that it can't be relied on for.

Targeting a series of numbers, specific words, or statements are examples of less than optimum targets for remote viewing. The way remote viewing works does not currently permit this degree of detail. It is probably because of the way the information is transferred. General ideas and concepts that can be formed based on many different (usually fractured) elements that are received from the target generally only permit gross conclusions or assumptions about the target.

Series of numbers, or specific words or phrases do occur, but only rarely, and then only when a collection of data bits permits. An example would be the name of a city that has a sufficient degree of uniqueness about it or perhaps the name of an important individual about whom quite a bit is known historically.

Remote viewing is generally not very good for providing information on mythical creatures, hypothetical events, non-physical properties, or phenomenological types of targets. In other words, it's generally not good for UFOs, the Lock Ness Monster, Sasquatch, or descriptions of heaven and hell (although I hope I stand corrected at some point about Sasquatch, and at least the data I've provided about UFOs to date.)

In determining if it can be used for any of these issues, one has to exercise a great deal of caution. In some cases, some things, that on the surface may seem to be over the edge when properly targeted, could actually produce a result.

As an example, up until the turn of the century, no westerner had ever seen a gorilla. Remote viewing, applied properly, could have reduced the search area considerably in the attempt to find one. However, I should also state that even though none had been seen, there was significant and abundant evidence that gorillas did exist. There were bones, hair samples, and other items available to western science that almost guaranteed they existed prior to one physically being located.

UFOs are another example. It would be one thing to target a specific location on the planet, one to which you could travel and properly check out. But using remote viewing to identify a UFO base on Jupiter or the dark side of the Moon is totally useless and probably a waste of time.

Contrary to general opinion, using remote viewing to

produce a location is also not a good idea. This is probably one of the least accurate ways of using this capability. While very precise descriptions of locations can generally be provided, remote viewing will usually not work very well unless there is something very unique about the location, or a general area is already known to exist. I know this will be sad news to those who are looking for a missing child, but unfortunately it is true. Finding something or someone works only where superior police or detective work has been married to the remote viewing ahead of time. This usually occurs when local law enforcement officials have spent a considerable amount of time in a crime area, and the object or person has not been moved a long distance from that location. In the case of a kidnapping resulting in a missing person, this usually means the victim is dead.

It is not difficult to understand that when it comes to search problems, finding a dead person is a lot easier than finding a live one. A missing person who keeps moving automatically compounds the problem every time they do.

Unreasonable Expectations

False expectations about what remote viewing can and can't do are generally born out of the re-mystification of remote viewing and its capabilities, usually by the media, but sometimes by people who claim to be remote viewers but who clearly do not understand what it really is.

These unreasonable expectations can be defined under the following major topics:

1. END USERS OF REMOTE VIEWING DATA.

Because they have no background in remote viewing, it is really not their fault if they expect too much from it. It is the viewer's responsibility to establish the boundaries or limits within which it can operate. If remote viewers over-sell their capability, they will never meet expectations. One of the easiest ways to oversell anything is to start telling people how good it is—even when it isn't.

Except for perhaps five occasions I know about in twenty-five years, I've never seen remote viewing exceed sixty-five percent reliability. These five occasions had to do with only two viewers, both of whom worked in the Cognitive Sciences Lab. In all five cases, time was not a factor, and the degree of excruciating detail, time and effort, to which these two viewers went to guarantee a 90 percent result, no one but a lab could afford. The old adage holds here. If it sounds too good to be true, it is.

It is the responsibility of the viewer to be honest about the remote viewing capability even if it hurts. If you do better than you've projected, then everyone will benefit. Being honest about the capability also gives the users of the information sufficient knowledge up front to appropriately plan for its use. This way, if additional technology needs to be brought on board, they don't find that out when it is too late.

2. THE REMOTE VIEWER.

The effectiveness of remote viewing has to be objectified. Therefore, people cannot evaluate their own material, because they are too close to it. When trying to determine just how good remote viewing is, there are many elements that come into play.

How much of what was said was correct? How much of what could have been said was actually said? How much of what was said was wrong?

In a lab there are long and tedious procedures for evaluating remote viewing. But in applications there are none. If remote viewers produce a minimal amount of information, but also provide the one thing the customer happens to be interested in, then it's considered highly successful. If the remote viewer produces volumes of correct information about the target, but fails to produce that single necessary element of data, it's a failure. During most application types of targeting, data is lost, destroyed, abandoned, or ignored. At best, it is squeezed into some form of report, which generally calls for a conclusion.

So, unless very specific targeting is done, to establish accuracy data on a viewer, it is almost impossible to make more than a general claim.

3. THE MEDIA.

If I were to pick the least authoritative source for details on accuracy it would be the media. The media is interested in one thing—sound bites. The more profound and sensational the sound bite, the better. They will quote something out of context in a heartbeat.

I remember one notable statement that exemplifies this capacity for inaccuracy. Dr. Edwin May appeared on the ABC Special, "Put to the Test", where he gave an interview and referred to some of my remote viewing. Somewhere in that interview he was commenting on the near-perfect match between some of my drawings and the target. His statement was something like, "Joe provides this kind of spectacular detail about twenty percent of the time. Scientists don't like to say this, but that's about as close to a miracle as one can get."

This statement was made along with other statements that reflected a target hit rate of about sixty to sixty-five percent. But in this statement, he was specifically referring to near perfect drawings, something that rarely happens in remote viewing.

Unfortunately, when it was edited, it was taken

completely out of context. This resulted in a huge negative reaction from other viewers, which was grossly unfair to both Ed and me. My recommendation is to never rely on the media for statements of accuracy.

The Weakness of Statistics

What can be expected from the *average* remote viewer is probably something about three times better than chance. Most good viewers will be able to make contact with a target about 50 to 60 percent of the time. When they do make contact, about 30 to 80 percent of what they say about the target could be correct. Notice, I said "could be." There is usually no way to know until the information has been used, checked, and verified against what can be known about the target. In applications, this process can sometimes take years.

Statistics don't really mean a thing to the customer who is in need of help and they most certainly don't mean a thing to the viewers who know that every remote viewing they do could either be near perfect, or a complete bust.

Statistics should only be developed within a lab, or during the *post hoc* analysis of research targets, when all of the variables are being controlled. The method of evaluation should be one that has been accepted.

The methods of evaluation are almost as prone to criticism as the remote viewing itself, so the method used should be one that has withstood the test of fire; that is, it should be one that has been accepted by a majority of the scientific community.

Chapter Four

A Remote Viewer's Mental State

It might seem kind of strange addressing the mental state of a remote viewer. Some think a belief in the possibility of remote viewing alone should be sufficient to question a person's sanity. But, this is not the kind of thing I want to talk about here. I'm referring to a person's ability to think critically and to maintain a healthy skepticism regarding the subject matter.

Original Concerns

Way back in the beginning, there was concern about a number of things in the STARGATE Project, but probably highest on the list was the stability of the players. This may sound strange. You would think finding people who are open to psychic functioning would be highest on the list. However, that is precisely the reason for taking care.

Reality dictates that if you want to start a project that will be investigating the use of psychics, you can't simply walk into the effort with people who believe in it. Nor, surprisingly, can you walk into the room with people who refuse to believe. What you end up with, in either case, are people who will find what they want to find. Both groups already have an *a priori* expectation for what they want to see. The people who have totally bought into it will be quick to jump to the conclusions necessary to support what they want to believe is happening versus looking for something else that might be going on instead. The ones who reject it out of hand won't recognize it when it's happening. Or, as in the case with some scientists I know, will only believe that there must be an information leakage path hidden somewhere in there, even though they can't seem to find it.

The kinds of people you need are those who are open to whatever the possibilities might be, but who also retain a very healthy and stiff resistance to accepting a paranormal explanation as a reality without substantial proof being offered.

Until my introduction to the subject matter, I did not know just how rare these kinds of individuals might be. Add in the fact that you are searching for people who are also talented or gifted in a psychic way, and you are beginning to understand the difficulty.

There are a number of complaints that one hears with great regularity from both sides of the issue. On the scientific side, they usually center on skepticism and what it means. Skepticism in the loose extreme can mean little or nothing, and in the opposite probably represents nothing more than a cover for a debunking exercise. Many don't understand that there is even a difference.

A person who attempts to debunk remote viewing is really someone trying to expose it as a sham or fraud. They enter the scene with a belief that remote viewing is a sham or fraud, so any pretense at being skeptical in a healthy sense of the word is shattered from the outset. Most people who take the role of debunkers are fanatical in their approach. They usually take the tack of attempting to show how it could be done through fraud, and generally do not pay any more attention to the protocols and scientific rules than someone who doesn't understand them in the first place. Even where fraud or deception is being used, debunking isn't necessary. An honest and skeptical approach and a requirement for enforcing protocol will expose it. In my opinion most debunkers or people who walk in the door with their mind made up are either in it for the money and the notoriety, or are operating from some deep-seated and personal fear about the subject matter. The term is inappropriately used when a scientist who is doing his job as an honest skeptic is improperly called a debunker by those who take exception to a well-founded and sincere scientific investigation.

A skeptic, on the other hand, usually suspends judgment or withholds it, waiting for the proof to appear. It is actually a doctrine that there is no such thing as true knowledge, that we will never really know the entire truth about something, but are doomed to study it and conjecture about it forever. It is therefore very possible for someone to be honestly skeptical about something or anything and still righteously study it in detail. In my own opinion, this should be the position of anyone working in the paranormal field. My best friends in the investigation of the paranormal are honest skeptics. They have a maddening way of seeing things that anyone tied to a belief system will miss. They ferret out possible information leakage paths that even the smartest investigator will sometimes miss. In most cases they send you back to the drawing board to produce protocols that are just about as airtight as one can make them. They *always* help and support the discovery process. Give me an honest skeptic any day over someone who's already made up his or her mind about something.

So why would a discussion about skepticism be essential to a chapter on a remote viewer's mental state?

Because, when you stray from healthy skepticism you enter an entirely different realm—the realm of the *believer*.

Paranormal phenomena have been around since the beginning of time. It's even been used by the military for almost as long as there's been a military (re: *The Psychic Battlefield: Psychics and Soldiers,* William Mandelbaum, St. Martin's Press, 1999), There is a lot of mystery and mythology that's grown around the use of psychics. Some of it's good and some is bad. When the effects on people are good, there's usually not a problem; when they are bad, things begin to fall apart rather rapidly.

In our current culture, paranormal subjects cut across both philosophic and religious ground. If you read the available and not too distant literature, you will find that many still regard parapsychologists as people who believe in spirits, possession, Akashic records, things that go bump in the night, and (shudder), even the existence of a God. The subject has not been able to shed its "dark ages" connections. When modern science was born or came into enlightenment as some have said, there was a major effort to disavow this connection. While this is probably not the place to argue the merits of such belief, it is still necessary to point out that many believers have strong philosophic and religious convictions, and refuse to break from the past.

As soon as you acknowledge this connection, you begin to dwell within a very gray area. It is one's philosophical and theological beliefs (or deficiencies as the case may be) that support one's ability to live with others, interact, integrate change, and deal with life's conditions. How you think in these two areas mediates the very thoughts that drive you. It is the origin of our motivations.

Our fears, guilt, happiness, depressions—even the way we relate to others is completely underpinned by these two subjects. Anything and everything we experience in connection with the paranormal has both minor and major impact on our philosophic or theological belief. It therefore changes our very nature. It alters the way we respond to crises, changes the very foundation of our understanding or belief in how conscientiousness operates, the way we relate to others, how we think about right and wrong, and it most definitely causes us to rethink the basic tenets surrounding cause and effect.

Even for those who have a very strong and healthy skepticism, who are able to walk the centerline, continually questioning the reality of what they might be experiencing, the impact is profound. Those who aren't mentally stable at the outset do not possess the critical thinking skills that can protect them from sudden and damaging change. It's only a matter of time until they are irrevocably damaged. You need only talk with any experienced clinical psychologist or psychiatrist to know that this is true. Once a significant stone of belief in someone's foundation has been destroyed, it is almost impossible to put it back together again. You don't have to destroy too many stones in people's structure to collapse their entire mental faculty.

Another reason why changes in philosophic and theological belief are important deals with the challenges of the subject matter itself.

The paranormal arena is filled with fraud—at least three kinds. The first is actually one of the easiest to detect—that would be deliberate fraud. If you are doing your homework and pursuing the paranormal in an appropriate and scientific manner, your protocol design, peer review, and experimental safeguards should detect most of it. Probably the greatest mistake that most people make is totally relying on those facts and assuming they've thought of everything. Well, guess what? They can't. The fact of the matter is, the world of the paranormal is filled with fraud. There is no doubt there are hundreds of people claiming to be psychic who are totally fraudulent and very good at it.

I long ago accepted the fact that in the study of parapsychology, one must *assume* there is going to be fraud and take proactive steps to prevent it. This means that in designing remote viewing protocols, you assume everyone is out to fix the results. Yes, that includes experimenters as well.

What about training?

It sort of cuts the other way. I would not assume the person training me (and collecting my money) is actually training me in something unless I knew there was no room for fraud on his behalf. Most trainers assume the person being trained wouldn't be cheating in some way, as they are honestly attempting to learn. Well, that may not be true.

In the labs in which I've worked, they will tell you right up front that they are designing the protocols to prevent fraud, and one shouldn't take it personally. I agree emphatically and I do not take it personally.

There is a second kind of fraud, which we can call accidental. I know, there are now lots of raised eyebrows out there. But, there are cases of information leakage in remote viewing experiments that support accidental fraud, or what could be construed as such. That would be where someone does something which s/he honestly believes is okay, simply because s/he's ignorant of the rules. Some psychics would believe that adding information after they've completed a project because they honestly were thinking the information at the time, but just didn't remember to write it down, is okay. Or, since it is an operational or applications type of target, it's okay to bend the rules. It's the end result that's important, right?

Dead wrong.

What happens is that it creates an atmosphere that strongly supports the third and most lethal form of fraud—which I call self-delusion. That's were you violate a significant number of smaller issues, allowing a false result, which contributes to altering your own belief that what you are doing is right. It is truly amazing how defensive people will get when you attempt to point out a possible leakage path that needs to be sealed, even when they know you are probably right. It's terribly difficult giving up a confirmed belief that what you are doing or have been doing is working, or that you are right and not wrong in whatever position you might have taken.

Self-delusion is seriously threatening to mental stability, especially when it begins to modify behavior. I have found myself strolling down that path on more than one occasion and suspect that I will find myself there again. It takes a great deal of effort, openness, and a dependence on others to tell you when you might be dealing with such an issue.

In my twenty plus years of dealing with conditions surrounding the field of the paranormal, I have seen numerous instances where seriously bad calls have been made. Almost without exception, these bad calls were a result of either not taking a person's mental state seriously or not recognizing the impact that exposure to the paranormal might have on a vulnerable individual. Not rank (military or civilian), age, experience, or previously displayed capability in other areas was a good pre-indicator for who could handle it and who could not. The outset of the STARGATE Project involved extensive psychological testing and numerous interviews, as well as a gradual program of exposure, to insure that centered and stable individuals were allowed to participate, individuals who could cope with and integrate what they would be exposed to. Terminating that approach has once again opened the door to this issue, the very least of which can result in self-delusion regarding remote viewing.

There is an argument to be made about all of what I just said. "This paranormal stuff is all exploratory and I am the master of my own mind, my own body, and my own sanity. No one should control what I'm exposed to, no more than they should control my freedom of religion."

This is absolutely correct.

The single reason for this entire chapter and everything I've said about it is simply to give a warning. The worst that can happen is that people will go off the deep end and actually become a victim of their own pursuit. The least is perhaps accidental fraud or self-delusion. But, this still needs to be addressed. It would be unethical to know that such a possibility exists and not pay any attention to it. It would be unconscionable for a lab or any other facility to expose someone who is obviously unstable to the effects such philosophic or theological impacting experiences might bring. It's a responsibility every scientist, trainer, and remote viewer must acknowledge and assume.

Chapter Five

---- ✴ ----

Who Makes a
Good Remote Viewer?

One of the greatest problems faced by any of us who wants to use or study the art of remote viewing, is finding the remote viewers. A considerable amount of information has appeared over the Internet, in advertisements, books, magazine articles, and other media that describes this process. Much of this describes how to identify who would make good remote viewers or what skills might be necessary in order to learn remote viewing. Advice ranges from "anyone can learn it" to "only those with a great deal of psychic talent are able to learn." While there is actually a bit of truth in just about everything you read, the context in which the statement is made actually determines its accuracy.

Back when the United States Army decided to find, train, and use remote viewers for Project STARGATE, no one knew what this meant. There were no books or articles that clearly outlined a method for finding someone who might be psychic, nor did any known method for training someone in remote viewing exist. The people attempting to organize and establish the project decided to let common sense drive them where they had to go. The first place they looked, of course, was SRI-International, where remote viewing had already been studied for nearly five years, and comments relative to training and gifted versus non-gifted subjects could be found.

What SRI-International Knew Back Then

Back in early 1978 there wasn't much known about the "common traits" that might be found in the typical psychic. Depending on whom you talked with, you might get any one of a number of answers, nearly all subjective.

Nevertheless, some comments relative to the subject can be found in one of the original publications relating to remote viewing: *A Perceptual Channel for Information Transfer over Kilometer Distances: Historical Perspective and Recent Research*. Harold E. Puthoff and Russell Targ, Member and Senior Member of the Institute of Electrical and Electronics Engineers, Inc., (IEEE) Annals No. 603PR004, 1976.

In the first few pages of their report, Hal and Russell state:

"The development at SRI of a successful experimental procedure to elicit this capability has evolved to the point where persons such as visiting government scientists and contract monitors, with no previous exposure to such concepts, have learned to perform well; and subjects who have trained over a one-year period have performed excellently under a variety of experimental conditions. Our accumulated data thus indicate that both specially selected and unselected persons can be assisted in developing remote perceptual abilities up to a level of useful information transfer."

Lest anyone immediately jump to a string of erroneous conclusions, there are a number of assumptions that the reader should *not* automatically make based on these statements. These are:

"Perform well," as it was used here, does not imply

world-class remote viewing, such as the kinds of examples that are held up for the media as examples of current remote viewing state-of-the-art. What they actually mean here is the ability to display psychic functioning under controlled conditions (or achieving a better than chance result).

Also, "subjects who have trained over a one-year period" did not automatically mean that they were taught some deeper secret or psychic ability no one else possessed. It simply meant, at the time, more exposure—or practice.

Of course, almost anyone who is allowed to practice something for a substantial period of time will show some improvement, if for no other reason than familiarity with the process.

Even though initially everyone understood that almost anyone walking in the door could display some degree of talent, what is not said within the document is that most of the people Hal and Russell worked with were the ones who:

a) Displayed some degree of talent from the outset.

b) Voluntarily chose to continue involvement out of a strong personal interest in the subject (which is obviously a form of self-selection).

We can learn from this that by pursuing experimental-data collection with the use of self-selected subjects, or subjects chosen because they initially tested as gifted, we would be emulating some of the more productive research methods used by others within the paranormal field.

What therefore becomes important is Hal and Russell's observations relevant to the common traits they found in the subjects they chose to work with, even though these may have been subjectively deduced at the time.

Going back and reading this publication with the intent of discovering some of these observations, one can find some very interesting tidbits.

Subject Traits

1. Subjects should have ability to process information within a high stimulation environment (e.g., a Gansfeld setting).

   A Gansfeld setting is a procedure where the subjects would relax while viewing a uniform source of illumination through halved ping-pong balls taped over their open eyes, while at the same time listening to relatively loud uniform auditory stimulation (white noise background sounds).

2. Subjects should be self-selected.

3. Subjects should be able to learn through example.

4. Subjects should be open to the probability of paranormal information transfer.

5. Subjects should be able to deal with public scrutiny, the negative reactions of society, and ridicule as well as failure.

6. Subjects should have an artistic talent capable of expressing their perceptions, e.g., drawing, sketching, etc. (We now know that "artistic talent" can mean anything, including painting a high quality picture verbally.)

7. Subjects should be capable of providing imaginative (out of the box) solutions to problems.

8. Subjects should demonstrate right brain specialization characteristics, such as a flair for musical rhythm and melody, or a higher creative sense for shape, form, and texture.

9. Subjects should have a preference for reporting non-analytic data over a need for producing function or naming the target.

Additional Information

An additional document which was available and known to have been used by Army STARGATE founders to identify possible remote viewing subjects was a paper published in the Journal of Communications titled *Psi Conducive States,* by William G. Braud, pp. 142-152 (1975). At the time, William Braud was an Associate Professor of Psychology at the University of Houston, Texas.

According to his findings from research into different areas of study, including altered states of consciousness, cognitive psychology, hemispheric studies, Eastern and esoteric philosophies, mystical tradition, and parapsychology, he suggested that what he called a "psi-conducive syndrome" did indeed exist, and that it "has seven major characteristics. Some of these characteristics (or 'syndromes') are physiological, some are psychological, and others are phenomenological."

While these depict specific psi-conducive states and not specific remote viewer characteristics, they do indirectly provide us with things we should be paying attention to or that might be necessary in a remote viewer. These are:

a. Subjects should be physically relaxed. *[Which means capable of controlling their stress.]*

b. There is a reduction in physical arousal or activation. *[Subjects should be able to slow their body responses and quiet their physiology.]*

c. There is a reduction in sensory input and processing. *[Subject should be able to eliminate outside distractions, or meditate.]*

NOTE: This may appear to contradict the highly stimulated environment referenced two paragraphs before (paragraph a.), but actually it doesn't. What Braud is talking about deals specifically with external distractions or stimuli that might capture or otherwise occupy the subject's attention; whereas the Gansfeld model is a procedure that effectively reduces sensory-perceptual, somatic, and cognitive "noise" interfering with the weaker psi-signals, thus encouraging psi performance.

d. Subjects should have an increased awareness of internal processes, feelings and images (including dreams and fantasy). *[In other words, be able to at least control what they do with the information, reduce their assumptions, and try to separate imagination from reality.]*

e. Psi functioning should decrease with "action mode/left hemispheric functioning" and increase with "receptive mode/right hemispheric functioning." *[Subjects must be able to center themselves receptively.]*

f. Subjects should have an altered view of the nature of the world. *[Time is an illusion, there is a unity and relationship between all things, good and evil are human concepts—which suggests at least a suspension of judgment and interpretation.]*

g. The act of psychic functioning must be (at least) momentarily important. *[The subject needs to have a strong motivation to achieve an outcome. This would imply an empathic bond with someone who has a need for the information.]*

The Military Input

To the above criteria, one would of course add common sense. Finding a psychic within a military structure is actually pretty easy. You look for someone who has repeatedly and consistently survived the impossible.

It is sort of like looking for that gas station that's never been robbed. In a computer run of gas stations, it will stand out like a white crow.

The military people tasked with finding psychics added their own list of possible indicators that would show up against a common military background. Some of these were:

1. Consistently successful whatever the task.

2. Liked by peers but considered different from the norm.

3. Generally operates outside normal boundaries.

4. Willing to pursue new avenues of approach.

5. Open to whatever works.

6. Capable of critical thought and unafraid to voice an opinion.

7. Highly and uniquely creative.

These were the general guidelines that were used to hunt down the original psychics used in the STARGATE program. Of course not all the above parameters were found in all the subjects, and not all the above parameters turned out to be completely accurate in terms of selection criteria. There were problems.

What I Now Believe Is True

I now know that when it comes to measuring specific traits or characteristics in human beings, there are no absolutes. Different characteristics and different combinations of characteristics when found in different people will mean different things, and almost always produce a different result. While some of these combinations might change the desirability of one person over another as a possible psychic or remote viewer, desirability really doesn't matter, nor does it equate to a display of skill.

Even so, some traits or characteristics are just too important to ignore. So, I will share what I believe is true about the aforementioned traits and characteristics and why this may be so. Understand that since this is based on personal observation it is highly subjective and should not be assumed as the final word in this regard.

Ability to Process Information within a High Stimulation Environment

This appears to be necessary for two reasons: because of how psychic information is probably being received, as well as what we automatically try to do with our processing.

Think of the canvas of the mind as being a forest. It's filled with trees—a lot of trees. Since the mind is so fertile, we can't stop the darn things from growing. These trees represent all of the mental processing distractions that could be taking place. Some of these trees are swaying one way (left to right) because we are thinking about them; the rest, or ones we are not thinking about, are swaying in an opposite direction (right to left.) Well, the psychic or remote viewing information we receive (since we aren't really thinking about it) gets lost in the right to left swaying trees. At the same time, we are also being distracted by a continual attempt at re-focusing on the trees swaying left to right. In order to recognize the arrival of remote viewing information, we need to do something that will cause all the other trees, or information that isn't remote viewing information, to sway opposite. There are two ways of doing this.

We can submerge ourselves in a background of generic stimulation or noise. This would be stimulation that has no meaning so all those trees sway in one direction. Or, we can do something with our consciousness that will fool it into thinking all the trees are going in one direction, usually by occupying the mind with something trivial, so it is occupied, but not so occupied that it won't recognize the incoming or psychic information.

This is kind of like looking for movement against the forest with our eyes. If you look directly at the forest you probably won't see the new tree when it suddenly pops into view. But, if you look with your peripheral vision, you probably will.

So, subjects who can teach themselves to operate automatically, while consciously being occupied with something trivial, will usually fare better at describing psychic trees.

The second important part to understanding how this works deals with processing. Once the psychic tree has been noticed, you should draw it exactly as it has been seen. No analysis is required. In other words, if you start thinking about it and/or logically analyzing it, then it will quickly turn into something other than what it arrived as.

Another way of saying this would be to say someone has suddenly stopped noticing all the background trees swaying in one direction, which almost automatically diffuses the outline of the psychic tree which then rapidly begins to change.

Think of it as a dual processing methodology, where you are trying to recognize things showing up on both sides of a fence simultaneously. As soon as you attempt to do more than that, you not only lose sight of both sides of the fence, you find you have already forgotten what information you'd gotten up to that point.

I know this sounds like an almost impossible task to accomplish, but there are numerous examples of our doing this in our everyday lives. Driving a car and listening to a radio news broadcast; cutting grass on a mower while thinking about something you are going to do later; talking with a friend while you are cooking dinner, are all good examples, as is walking point in combat. One minute you are totally focused on a trail, and the next you are suddenly in a crouch with a full flight of butterflies in your stomach. Why? You just know.

Subjects Are Self Selected

This has absolutely no impact on someone's ability to display remote viewing talent or capability. However, it can be monumentally important when determining the psychological stability of a possible subject for training or for other reasons. I will go much deeper into this later in this chapter.

Subjects Should Be Able to Learn through Example

This sounds like no big deal, but it can be. There are a lot of people who are already deeply involved in the paranormal field. Most of these people have never seen a real remote viewing protocol. (I'm not talking about methodology here—but protocol.)

One of the keys to successful remote viewing is emulating a good practice—following protocol. If you think you can walk in the door and do it "your own way" and do a lot better, good luck.

Someone unable to set aside his or her belief structure as to how remote viewing information gathering might operate is probably in for Mr. Toad's wild ride, but they definitely won't be learning much about remote viewing.

Subjects Should Be Open to the Probability of Paranormal Information Transfer

If you close your mind to the possibility, then no matter how hard you try, you probably won't succeed. It doesn't take a rocket scientist to understand that someone who refuses to believe a bike can be ridden is highly unlikely to ride a bike.

This should not be confused with someone who might not think remote viewing is real, but is open to the possibility. I know dozens of avowed and honest skeptics who stated up front their disbelief. Entering the experimental process with an open mind quickly changed their viewpoint.

I have seen closed minds convinced, but not very often. Usually claiming to be completely closed to the idea, they themselves have demonstrated psi-missing. (That's violating chance in the opposite direction. Something akin to having told someone that they are psychic if they can call heads on a flipped coin 90 out of a 100 times—and trying so hard not to, they flip the tails side up 85 out of a 100 instead.)

Subjects Should Be Able to Deal with Public Scrutiny, Negative Reactions of Society, and Ridicule, as Well as Failure

This probably doesn't matter in terms of displaying talent as a remote viewer, at least initially. However, over time, it will wear a remote viewer down, especially the dealing with failure part.

Most people can deal with quite a lot of abuse if they are doing something they like to do. But, one element feeds on another. If you are not well supported by your little section of humanity or your social infrastructure, you will see it reflected in your failure rate. It doesn't take long before expectancy for failure begins to run you life. It also in turn feeds the social rejection syndrome. So these issues are inter-supportive of one another and over time can prove to be devastating. Kind of like being under a slow acid drip.

One needs either to have a thick skin when entering the process or be able to develop one along the way.

Society and culture might be unfair on the subject of remote viewing, but such scrutiny actually performs a function. As a remote viewer, if you can weather the broadsides from outside the system you will find you can weather just about anything. It performs much the same function as in the tempering of steel with fire and water. What comes out the other end is flexible and has an ability to deal with a lot of punishment while getting a job done.

Subjects Should Have an Artistic Talent

This was, in part, born out of a belief that the best way to display remote viewing information is through drawing.

Initially remote viewing centered around an ability to sketch or draw well. There was comment in the IEEE report that suggested that people who could draw were better remote viewers ("....drawings they make are in general more accurate than their verbal description." p. 337).

We now know that this isn't true in the way it was implied. However, artistic ability does seem important for other reasons. It's obvious that the more able you are to relate information in a number of different media, the better you will communicate that information.

At the beginning of the project, all of the methods for evaluating or judging the material were tuned to drawings. Drawings spoke louder than words. If you were looking at the Grand Canyon and held a drawing of canyons up next to it, it had a great deal more impact on the judges or skeptics, than if you simply said "very large hole in ground."

Nowadays there are many valuable ways of communicating information received through remote viewing. Aside from drawing, one of the most valuable is modeling the target in clay, or building it from scratch. A 3-D display of a target element really talks. However, verbal descriptions can be of immense value too, if one takes the time to study and understand how they are used by a specific remote viewer. One viewer may mean nothing with the statement "awesome burst of light," because they use it for almost anything. But, another viewer might only use that phrase when confronted with a coherent light beam (laser). This is why long-term relationships between specific viewers and specific Analysts become almost as important as any other part of the viewing process. I can almost guarantee doubling the accuracy of a viewer when such a relationship between a viewer and Analyst exists.

The key to degree of artistic talent required really falls on the term "consistency" more than any other thing. Someone who draws stick figures for people may not provide the detail someone else provides; but if they are consistently correct when they imply people present at the target, then the stick figures attain a much greater degree of importance. Someone may draw a human very close to scale and display human form nearly perfectly, but if they can't place the person correctly in the perceived room, it's of no value.

Subjects Should Be Capable of Providing Imaginative (Out of the Box) Solutions to Problems

This could be desirable for reducing remote viewing training time, but it isn't necessary. The very art of remote viewing if taught and learned properly produces this kind of a person.

Subjects Should Demonstrate Right Brain Specialization Characteristics

Back in the bad old days, this made sense. It no longer does, in my opinion—except perhaps allegorically. We now know that where something takes place in the brain probably isn't as important as the modality of thinking being used by the person.

A better way of wording this would be to say that someone who wants to be a remote viewer should have balance—should always fall somewhere in the middle. (I know you are scratching your head now. "Fall in the middle? What does he mean by that?")

It means, a remote viewer is totally open to any possibility—female or male, night or day, open or closed, inside or outside, up or down, etc. If you can't presume to be on either end of a stick, then you must always be in the middle.

This also ties directly to belief. If you have to always be in the middle in order to sit at an optimum starting point for psychic perception, then you can't believe anything that will put you on one end or the other. Remote viewers have to be so "neutral" that they flow like water wherever they have to flow in order to seek ground truth. Adding a single thought or desire as to where that should be, or how it might be, will automatically put them somewhere else.

Not too much right-brain, not too much left-brain, but right in the middle.

Subjects Need to Be Relaxed

Obviously this requires the ability to become mentally relaxed. However, this is something that can be learned.

I am a triple A-type personality, but when I want to be, I can look and act like grass growing. It is not an easy thing to manage, especially when you've just walked in the door after three hours of fighting traffic, or you just left the monthly planning conference. But, one can learn.

Almost any form of meditation works in this regard. If you can learn to meditate, you may learn to be a good remote viewer. If you can't, learn to race cars or play racketball to your heart's content, but don't waste your time on remote viewing.

Subjects Should Be Able to Reduce Their Physical Arousal Level

This has to do with focus, or the ability to cut out distractions that might occur while remote viewing. Another way of stating this is: viewers disassociate from what's around them and associate with the actual target site, person, object, or event. They actually mentally cease to be in the room where the distraction might be taking place. Again, it is something that can be learned and doesn't have to come at the outset.

Subjects Should Be Able to Reduce Sensory Input

This simply means shutting out audio or visual interference through an ability to focus. We do this all the time. Anyone with kids (any ages) who can carry on a conversation with their spouse at the dinner table, watch and understand the evening news, or think about a shopping list while driving them to the ball park understands what I'm talking about here.

Again, it's a talent that can be learned and does not have to be present when deciding if you are a remote viewer or not.

Subjects Should Have an Increased Awareness of Internal Processes, Feelings, and Images

If you do not currently have a general understanding for why you are depressed, angry, frustrated, anxious, bored, or in any other mental state, then you probably are going to have a very tough time with remote viewing.

One of the major keys to being a remote viewer is being able to look inside and study how and why you process or think the way you do. You need to be a clear and critical thinker, or you will face problems that may be insurmountable. Remote viewing requires being able to at least learn to control some of your most intimate mental and emotional processing functions.

PSI Functioning Should Decrease With "Action Mode/ Left Hemispheric Functioning" and Increase with "Receptive Mode/Right Hemispheric Functioning"

This was largely addressed already, but I would add once again, that I would separate action modes and receptive modes of thinking from the concept of right and left hemispheric functioning. I think they are two separate issues and do not operate as closely in unison as some believe.

Certainly, facilitating being in a receptive mode versus an action mode will go a long way to allowing remote viewing to operate. Most people can learn this through practice and it is not necessarily a characteristic that needs to exist from the outset.

Subjects Should Have an Altered View of the Nature of the World

Absolutely! This is definitely a requirement I would put at the head of the list. I am sure that time and space in their entirety are illusions, and these very illusions are why all things are related. There is no good or evil involved in remote viewing. There may be yin and yang, constructive and destructive energies, but good or bad exist only within the mind.

Now please note that I did not say that good and evil do not exist for me. They do. But I am saying that you cannot carry these concepts into remote viewing with you. By doing so, you build walls, construct tunnels, and essentially attempt to steer yourself to the information, instead of letting it just fall into your mind's hands. I could fill a medium-sized book with just my own arguments regarding good and evil. At the moment you will have to take my word for it.

It is absolutely essential that remote viewers suspend judgment and interpretation of the materials and information they might be receiving. Otherwise, everything you perceive will be tainted with the color of your desire, or shaded by the darkened glass of personal prejudice.

I know, I know. Some of you out there honestly believe you don't have a prejudiced bone in your body. Well, have I got news for you! Eliminating the last vestige of your personal prejudice is probably more difficult than performing open-heart surgery on yourself. And I can tell you I would not like to have to do that.

The best anyone can do is to temporarily set prejudice aside. And speaking from experience, that takes years of practice. Think of personal prejudice as how we like things to be. As an example; I am comfortable with the idea that grass is green. However, when I go into a remote viewing, I am comfortable with the idea that grass may not be real; I have to be. I think you get my drift.

If you are unable to set your personal wants, desires, likes, dislikes, etc., aside, then you are highly unlikely to make a good remote viewer.

The Act of Psychic Functioning Must Be (at Least) Momentarily Important

This is critically important to the success of any remote

viewing. However, having said that, I must add that it is not really my problem as a remote viewer.

Take note, all you scientists, researchers, and applications-oriented people out there; it's up to you to keep me interested, make sure the results are important to me, and not the other way around. You can do this a number of ways:

1. The types of targets used and their contents.

2. The reasons you give me for doing the remote viewing.

   a. It's importance from a social, historical, cultural, or survival viewpoint, or

   b. You pay sufficiently to buy my interest in the inevitable outcome, or

   c. Ensure that success provides some other form of reward that is intrinsic to the effort (finding a lost child, kidnap victim, or similar sort of thing).

There are probably more exotic ways, but I dare not put them into this book.

The idea here is that the remote viewer must share in or enjoy the value and reward that comes with success.

Must Be Consistently Successful at Whatever Task

There are myriad ways to measure success. How people value themselves is of key importance. If they consider themselves to be successful, to be valuable, then it doesn't matter how society or culture might measure success. Such people, secure in their own perceptions, will be better able to deal with the kinds of treatment they are bound to receive from the outside world. This is especially true about remote viewers. So, it's how they feel inside and their comfort level with themselves that counts.

Remote Viewing Secrets

Liked by Peers but Considered Different from the Norm

This characteristic works when you have a baseline of comparison. In the military, where you have a large percentage of conformists, this characteristic might have just a tad bit more value. It can also be valuable in a corporate world where you have people who buck the system but still seem to enjoy a large degree of success. However, for the average person this will probably have no meaning, as they are not trying to keep up with the Joneses, and really are kind of mellow about the whole thing, or whatever might be going on. These are people who are not satisfied with doing the job the way they were taught to do it. They seek out new ways to get the job done and actually do it better.

Generally Operates outside Normal Boundaries

Again, as in the above paragraph, this would be important, but only in comparison with an overall baseline. One should look for a person who consistently demonstrates an ability to find solutions to problems that are not within the norm, or might never have been tried before. Or, maybe a demonstration of actions that are totally unexpected but successful anyway.

Willingness to Pursue New Avenues of Approach

This is important from the standpoint of being open. If people decide up front that there are only very delineated or structured approaches to problems, then they are not open enough to enjoy remote viewing success. This ties in to the premise that deals with personal prejudices.

Open to Whatever Works

In the land of remote viewing, anything is possible. It is usually the surprising information that proves to be correct. The more open someone is to any possibility and the least wedded they are to a fixed reality, the more likelihood of success.

Highly and Uniquely Creative

I've deliberately addressed this characteristic out of order, since I want to really emphasize the last characteristic in this chapter. However, this one is just as important.

Someone who is very creative is already half way toward being a good remote viewer. Creative individuals have an instinct that they cherish above all other skills. This is the same instinct that inherently drives a remote viewer to the right answer. The right answer more times than not is going to be unique.

But this is also a chicken and egg problem. Which comes first—the good remote viewer or the creative problem solver? There really is no answer. And it really doesn't matter. I believe wherever you find a very creative and successful person, you will also find good material for remote viewing. They are already practicing what they need to learn.

Of course, if someone is able to learn how to be creative while at the same time learning remote viewing, then s/he clearly wins both ways.

Capable of Critical Thought and Unafraid to Voice an Opinion

Believe it or not, this is probably one of the most important qualifications. It's important because this is an active display of a person's individuality and internalized strength. By retaining their critical thought in all ways, they are by nature taking the "middle ground" on most issues. Remember how important I said that was?

Aside from the Above, Who Should Not Be a Remote Viewer?

There are two kinds of people who generally make terrible remote viewers: ones who under no condition will believe in it, and those who totally buy into it; no questions asked.

We even have a saying that's passed around the lab. "The worst possible participants are the believers." This means people who have become involved in remote viewing who have replaced their critical thinking ability with unquestioned belief.

Historically more damage has been done to remote viewing applications, research, and development by those who have bought it "no questions asked" than by all deliberate assaults on it from outside antagonists.

Critical thinking is essential to ensuring that both applications and research are polished and perfected beyond reproach. Critical thinking is essential to appropriately limiting how and when remote viewing might be used. And critical thinking is essential to weeding out erroneous beliefs, fraud, or any of the other thousands of things that can bring discredit on the field at large.

All scientists like to think of themselves as critical thinkers, but I will tell you that they are just as likely to lose their critical thinking ability as the next person. Everyone who participates in remote viewing applications or research has the responsibility to continually challenge the techniques, methods, protocols, testing, evaluations, reporting, and the participants' actions with a critical eye towards improving and perfecting the methods. If we fail in this task, then we might as well all quit and go home now.

Another type of person who should not become involved in remote viewing is someone who is not completely stable. This doesn't necessarily mean crazy, either. A lot of people are quite stable and dependable— when involved in areas of endeavor where they are comfortable.

In the military we have people who function quite comfortably within the confines and constraints of normal military jobs and living. But, when moved into the paranormal arena, they lose their connection with real world boundaries that are necessary for their continued stability. At the outset of the military STARGATE Program, great effort was made to insure that stability. But testing, multiple interviews, and a long term vetting process is very expensive. Later in the program, a decision was made to no longer do this testing in order to reduce costs. Without going into specific personalities, I can say that in more than one case, otherwise stable individuals were stripped of their psychological boundaries, and subjected to areas of inquiry that they should not have been. As a result they became quite unstable, emotionally, mentally, or sometimes both. The field is still struggling with the damage resulting from these individuals' experiences. It is unfortunate for both the field as well as the people who suffered as a result.

As far as I can see there are no controls whatsoever on who becomes involved in remote viewing in the public arena. Individuals are welcomed through the door, enter sometimes unproven training programs, and are otherwise exposed carte-blanche to processes that unhinge them from their stable environs. A few ex-military viewers I know attempt to influence and screen those they feel might be damaged by involvement in remote viewing, but even so, this is not done unless the person wanting to participate is overtly acting out in some fashion that warrants exclusion. And, unfortunately, many who now claim expertise in this field make no attempt at all to screen participants.

About twenty percent of the people who contact me through my office at Intuitive Intelligence Applications are looking for help in regaining their stable pre-exposure attitudes. Since I am not a psychiatrist or psychologist, I am forced to refer them to qualified counsellors for help.

I'm not sure how anyone could tell subjectively whether or not s/he will have an adverse reaction through exposure to remote viewing. One way, of course, would be to ask yourself if you have a personal fear regarding the subject. If yes, then it is probably not a good idea to become involved.

Another indication would be an inability to think critically about the subject. If you can't enter with a healthy skepticism, then your boundaries are probably not sufficiently established to protect you from the consequences.

Of course, irrational or absolute belief (as in, "I know this is true!") about things that are not yet proven might be another indication that one's boundaries are not what they should be.

Obvious things like hearing voices, etc., are not really as obvious as they might seem. It usually takes a professional to determine the differences between someone who is probably crazy and someone who is pleasingly eccentric or just plain strange and different. These are all questions that revolve around who should and who should not become involved in remote viewing. Many really don't want to hear this in discussion, as it may come across as elitist, detrimental, controlling, or perhaps even be seen as finger-pointing and judgmental. Nevertheless, it is crucial to the subject at hand. It is the responsibility of those already involved in remote viewing to evaluate a possible participant prior to exposure, not the participant's requirement to suddenly determine their own instability post initiation.

Determining the Probable Skill Level of a Remote Viewer

There is only one way I know of doing this. It's called testing. You demonstrate what remote viewing is and how it works to the individuals and then test them coming in the door. What they display in terms of talent is probably somewhere between fifty and one hundred percent of what they will eventually display after training. Most scientists I know agree with this statement. The ones that don't will usually say something like, "What you see is what you get." In other words, they have no expectancy for improvement of any kind through training.

Obviously I do not believe in the latter statement, or I would not be writing this book. What I have observed over twenty plus years is something like the following: If people are brought into remote viewing and shown encouraging examples of a remote viewer who is successful, and time is spent building confidence in the probability of remote viewing working, then, when tested, they will usually perform well from the outset. Over time, with almost any training system that stresses a methodology that's used within an appropriate protocol, they will attain polish and more confidence in their ability, and there will be some improvement. However, that improvement will usually range from minimal to probably less than fifty percent of what they walked in the door with as innate or natural talent.

So, appropriate subject selection or testing at the fore goes a long way towards identifying those individuals one might consider gifted. Overall, while gifted individuals will usually range around one-half of one percent of any given population, almost anyone (the balance of any given population) can demonstrate fairly consistent results sufficient to show functioning beyond chance. Many may lose their interest over time, as a function of losing sight of its relative importance within their lives.

But as almost anyone can be a black belt in karate, the same holds true for RV'do. All it really takes is a strong desire to succeed, sustained over a fairly long learning curve.

Chapter Six

✸

Protocols and Methodologies, What They Are, and Why They Are Different

Lots of arguments have evolved over the past few years regarding these two subjects and as a result have produced lots of new mythology and confusion. It is a difficult issue to understand, but I would like to try to make it a bit easier.

It would be a mistake to say that the difference lies simply between what scientists believe and what others believe. I've met as many scientists who don't understand what a proper protocol is, as non-scientists who do. So you can't really make that kind of an assumption here.

Merriam Webster's Collegiate Dictionary, Tenth Edition, defines a *protocol*, as it applies here as: "a detailed plan of a scientific or medical experiment, treatment, or procedure."

However, it lists a *methodology* as: "a body of methods, rules, and postulates employed by a discipline: a particular procedure or set of procedures." As a secondary definition it gives: "the analysis of the principles or procedures of inquiry in a particular field."

It certainly isn't difficult to see why these two terms are

commonly mixed and/or interchanged in the remote-viewing field. So why does it matter a hill of beans, if we are talking about a procedure in either case?

The problem lies in the use of the term "scientific" in conjunction with remote viewing. If you are going to claim the fact that something is different for "scientific reasons," from something that would otherwise look and smell the same, then you have to define what makes that difference "scientifically." You do this with a protocol and not a methodology (or approach).

If you remove the specific protocols that have developed around remote viewing for the past twenty-five years, you are left with a very generic something, called "psychic functioning." Many don't remember the reasons for using the term remote viewing versus any other *nom-de-plume*, but I do. It was specifically done to identify something that was far and away removed from any other form of psychic functioning. Referring to remote viewing protocols as methods does a major disservice to the original studies, research, and intent.

Quite a few methods have grown out of the remote viewing culture that are not well seated in proven scientific protocols, and can't be called scientific by any stretch of the imagination. Since that is true, their continued success becomes almost solely dependent upon a waffling of the terms. I guess some figure, "After all, the average guy on the street won't know the difference." And to be frank, the average guy on the street doesn't.

The Basic Scientific Protocols, How They're Implemented and Why

The basic scientific types of protocols were designed to address real world or physical targets in the past, present, or future. These might include places, objects, people, events, technology, or photographs, all of which might either be stationary (fixed in place) or moving, indoor or outdoor, close-by or a long way off.

Protocols developed within the military during Project STARGATE stretched many of these well known protocols to address additional areas that include ideas, concepts, plans, thoughts, feelings, and/or emotions as targets.

Areas that were not formally addressed, by either the military, or the scientists, are the types of targets that remain largely in an "unknown category," such as; space type targets, mythology based concepts, and of course, aliens.

Unfortunately, rumors now run rampant regarding these latter kinds of targets and the use of remote viewing for ferreting out information about them. With few exceptions, the only reason remote viewing might have ever been attempted in the first place on such targets was because of the personal interest among viewers. In truth, the possibility of ever producing verifiable information on such targets is remote in the extreme.

Physical or Real World Targeting

This can be easily identified from published documentation in scientific journals, most of which as been done over the past twenty-five years. Real world targets have the fullest range in difficulty, the kinds of information they produce, and certainly in the way they are accomplished. The following provides a brief outline of some of the more important types of physical target protocols:

Outbounder Targets
Historically this is the baseline protocol that brought notoriety to remote viewing following publication in the IEEE by Hal Puthoff and Russell Targ in 1976.

1. Participants in this protocol are as follows:

a. **A Person Who Decides What the Target Is.** This is someone who is not otherwise associated with the remote viewers or anyone else directly involved in the remote viewing effort. It is the person who establishes the target pool. In the case of research or study, the person who creates the pool should not have any contact whatsoever with anyone else involved in the remote viewing effort. This precludes any possible contamination or sensory leakage to either the remote viewer, or the judges involved in performing or evaluating the remote viewing. In a case where it might be used in an application, the person who creates the pool usually has no direct contact with the remote viewer. There is usually a middle person who handles the targeting materials between the person who runs the pool (or targets) and the viewer.

b. **A Remote Viewer.** This is the person who actually does the remote viewing and produces the psychic information (this is also where you will find people who largely talk about and describe their methodologies and not the actual protocol[s]).

c. **A Monitor.** It isn't always necessary, but sometimes there is an additional person with the viewer while the remote viewing is going on. This person's title might be determined by what s/he might be doing. For now we will simply call them monitors. Monitors sit with viewers while they are doing remote viewing. They really aren't monitoring in the purest sense of the word, but are there for one of two reasons. If it is a remote viewing for research or study, then the monitor sees that the protocol is being adhered to, and that there is no fraud or mistakes in protocol that might interfere with the study. Monitors might take care of other things like recording of data, time and record keeping, perhaps bio-monitoring chores, that sort of thing. If the remote viewing is for an application purpose, or to collect information for someone, then the monitor is there to see that the remote viewer doesn't stray from protocol, or in some cases to help the viewer with the specific collection methodology. In any case, the monitor is never there to guide, lead, imply, or otherwise interfere with what the remote viewer is doing. Nor is the monitor there to provide information to the viewer. There is a way of using the monitor to provide minimal guidance, but since this deals with front-loading issues, it is more thoroughly covered in Chapter Eight.

d. **An Outbounder.** Of course, this is the person who physically visits the target site, and acts as the target individual or beacon. The Outbounder's job is to simply interact with the site and in that way, provide an address to the target by his or her presence. Some believe the Outbounder is there to pass telepathic information back to the viewer, but this is probably wrong. While telepathic information transfer is certainly taking place, so are many other forms of communication. If an Outbounder were being used for an applications type of target (which would be rare), if telepathic communications is all we are trying to accomplish, why add the additional cognitive filter of remote viewing? That wouldn't make any sense. Usually, a viewer will provide a considerable amount of information that the Outbounder never has direct access to on the target site.

e. **An Evaluator (Analyst).** The last person in an Outbounder protocol is the person who evaluates the material. In the case of research or study, this is the person who judges the material and determines through a strictly designed and pre-determined evaluation system whether or not remote viewing or a transfer of information has actually taken place. In the case of an application, this is the Analyst who checks to see if the pre-determined questions have been answered. In either case, the evaluator should have no contact with any member of the out bounder team until after evaluations or analyses have been made and no other visits to the target site are intended.

2. A protocol flow chart and timing sheet is provided in Appendix D.

Targeting with Coordinates

There is myth about how and why coordinates have come to be used. Some of it is true and some isn't. The following is my understanding of the reasons behind it, as related to me by most of the people involved.

Initially, the Outbounder protocol was used exclusively by the SRI-International scientists. Obviously because they were achieving such remarkable results, there was no hurried attempt to change it. But eventually it began to raise some difficulties.

While the San Francisco Bay area offers a wealth of possible targets locations, after the subjects have worked the area for some time, they begin to become bored with the target pool. Also, scientific questions begin to arise as to what else might affect remote viewing. Is distance to the target a factor? Is loss of information an effect of differences in time zones? That kind of thing. So, a different methodology for targeting needed to be devised. But, how do you get remote viewers to focus on a specific place or event that's totally remote from their location when you don't have someone standing there acting as a beacon?

It's true, they could still send an outbounder to the site (which could be half way around the world), but the expense over time would be enormous. Also, one needs to remember that there was considerable interest in remote viewing by certain intelligence agencies. This presented certain types of target opportunities that no one might have access to.

As I understand it, one of the psychics working at the lab, Ingo Swann, suggested the answer. They could use map coordinates to identify a specific location on the ground. Hence was born what is now known as the "coordinate system."

The initial targets selected and identified by coordinates were large geographic features, such as islands, rivers, mountains, waterfalls, cityscapes, and the like. To everyone's surprise, it worked just as well as the outbounder protocol.

There were some problems, however. It didn't take long for skeptics to begin clamoring about eidetic memory. This alleged that remote viewers could have memorized (at least unconsciously) all of the major land features that can be identified from topographical maps, by their longitude and latitude gridlines. (I interpret this as a nice way of saying we were all cheating. Which of course we weren't.)

In any event, the use of coordinates also appealed to the military, especially for their types of targets (airfields, bunkers, buildings, etc.) So, to deal with the skeptical issues, the military side of the house did what the military does best—they improvised. Instead of using standard grid coordinates that anyone can read, they used military maps, which use a different coordinate system. Instead of 29 Degrees, 37 minutes, 15 seconds North, by 082 Degrees, 22 minutes, 11 seconds West; it might read something like, HM 3487 9864. Based on the specific military map being used, both the letters and the number combinations constantly change with no real logical order. To our surprise, it worked just as well, but there were still complaints about eidetic memory. After all we were "military remote viewers."

So, at least on the military side, we began putting the real map coordinates inside sealed and opaque envelopes, and then we would write false coordinates on the outside. Since they were false coordinates, we simply left off the degrees, minutes, and seconds. The coordinates that were visible looked something like, 457816 987602. Point being, they really had no actual meaning, other than to identify that day's project. To no one's real surprise, the remote viewer still went to the intended target with very little trouble.

The target coordinates quickly became almost anything that was written on the exterior of the envelope that might continue to differentiate one target from another. As long as they say nothing about the character or content of the target of interest identified within, almost anything can be used as an identifier label or coordinate without.

There are only two differences between the outbounder type of protocol and the coordinate protocol:

1. There is no outbounder. Someone still decides what the target will be, but, instead of handing the target to an outbounder, s/he instead seals the targeting specifics inside an opaque envelope and then writes an identifying coordinate on the outside. In the case of research or study, the envelope is never given to the monitor or viewer. Only the identifying "coordinate" is. In the case of an application type of target, it generally doesn't matter, as what is being done is not being done for scientific record, but is being done to obtain information. Participants realize that violating the protocol by tampering with the envelope will only preclude information collection and spoil the data collected.

2. The other difference is in the feedback for the target. Since there is no outbounder site that the remote viewer can visit for feedback after the remote viewing has been completed and information evaluated, it becomes necessary to provide the viewer with as much

information as is feasible about the original target after the remote viewing has been completed. The person who controls the targeting information or the target pool is usually the person tasked with this.

All the other elements found within the outbounder protocol remain the same for the coordinate protocol. An example of a protocol flow chart and timing sheet are provided in Appendix D.

As you can already see, very little in the original protocol is being changed. Only the parts dealing with getting the viewer to the right target is being modified. One could argue feedback as well, but since feedback never takes place as long as a remote viewing target is active or being evaluated, it probably doesn't matter.

This now brings us to photographic target protocols.

Photographic Targets

This is where research and applications took distinctly different paths. There are a lot of different ways to use photographs as a targeting mechanism. Each one requires a detailed adherence to a specific protocol or procedure. Since I could actually write a book on photographic targeting alone, I will stick to the central issues, which are: differences between research types of targeting and applications targeting. What, and how much of what, do you allow the viewer to see.

1. Research and study targets.

This one I'll do first because it's the easiest. The simple rule is: if you are using photographs as targets, then they are *never* shown to the viewer till after the remote viewing has been completed, and the results have been evaluated. When used as targets, they can be sealed within an opaque envelope and given an identity number that is then used as a targeting mechanism, just as in the coordinate system. They can also be stored in a way that prevents viewing them until the remote viewing and evaluation has been accomplished, such as inside a computer file where they have been given coded identity numbers. The coded number is provided to the viewer, but not the photograph, until viewing and evaluation has taken place and the results filed. In research and study, there are no variations on this theme. The reason is because the photograph itself is the target (or at least is a paper representation of the location, object, person, or event).

2. Applications targets.

This is very different from research use of photographs. In this case the photograph is not generally the target, but is one step removed from it. In other words, the photograph is used to get a viewer to a specific target or element within the target that might be of greater interest.

There are lots of ways to use photographs to get a remote viewer to a target. However, each way presents a change in the basic protocol, so extreme care must be taken when handling photographs as targeting material.

Using Personal Photographs:

You can use photographs of people as unwitting outbounders. In the case of wanting to know "where" a missing person might be, since there is absolutely no way the viewer can know this information anyway, showing the actual photograph of the individual to the viewer is probably okay. It wouldn't be okay if you were going to ask the viewer something about the person that might be derived from the photograph. Photographs of individuals known to be in an area of interest would be another reason for showing the viewer a photograph of an individual, but you should never tell the viewer specifically what you are interested in with regard to the area.

Using Other Photographs:

It is actually easier to state what a remote viewer shouldn't see rather than what they should, as it is always a judgment call. Viewers should not be shown photographs of the specific target of interest. If you are interested in what's going on inside a building, you do not show the viewer (or monitor) a photograph of the building. If you are interested in what someone might be carrying in a briefcase, you don't show the viewer a picture of the briefcase. Everyone automatically wants to argue; why not? Well, one of the beautiful things about remote viewing is a viewer's ability to provide what otherwise would be very surprising information. But this can only be done when they have not been steered into some sort of expectancy, or their boundaries have not been perceptively fenced. If your interest is in what the person is doing who is carrying the briefcase, your assumption that the briefcase might contain information pertinent to that interest may be false. By showing viewers a photograph of the briefcase, you will encourage them to limit their perceptions to only the contents of a briefcase, or what might fit within it. In fact, anything the viewer does in reference to this target from that day forward will be mediated by what they feel about briefcases and their possible contents. It would be better to cut a very small square from that photograph that depicts the person's face, and ask what the person is doing.

To shorten what would otherwise be an inordinately long chapter in this book I will suggest the following rules when using photographs:

1. Always provide as little as possible in the way of photographs to a viewer. You can always go back later and expand on what you may be providing, but you can never undo what someone has already seen.

2. If a photograph implies anything at all about what you

might be interested in, put it in a sealed envelope and give it a coordinate.

3. Don't assume that because you can't ferret out information from a photograph, the remote viewer can't either. Most really good remote viewers are a lot more sensitive to information in photographs than the average person.

4. Above all else, never assume a photograph is the most accurate way to target a remote viewer. Whatever limits the photograph may also limit the viewer; that is, fence them in psychologically with regard to other possibilities or information.

Moving Targets

Outbounder, coordinate, or photographic targets can all be affected when the target is mobile. Unless there is a very clear description given by the viewer of a car, bus, train, plane, boat, etc., it is nearly impossible to evaluate a target while it is moving. The solution of course is to stop it from doing so.

A variation in location can only occur across time. A moving target therefore almost always requires multiple remote viewings at different times, and you must always use targeting material that is itself moving. A kidnap victim is sometimes moved frequently. Therefore it would be a good idea to use a photograph of the victim as targeting material and not something that might have been there at the time of the kidnap, like a victim's car or purse.

Those who are analyzing the remote viewing material should be told that there is a possibility that the target is a mobile target. Otherwise, they will assume—because elements of information they might be providing do not seem to be connected, one element to another—that what they perceive must be wrong. This is one of the few times the Analyst should be told something about the target.

Clock speed is not material to the efficacy of using remote viewing. What this means is any derivative or function of time can be used. For example:

1. Describe the target at noon over a four-day period.

2. Describe the target in 30-minute intervals.

3. Describe the target in one-second hops.

4. Describe the target's change in four even increments from 10^{-12} through 10^{-13} centimeters.

In these examples, the viewer can be told the specific tasking (1-4), as long as the target is being targeted through the outbounder, coordinate, or photographic (sealed envelope) protocols.

Non-Physical Targets

Obviously these preclude the use of the Outbounder protocol, unless possibly you are targeting someone who was supposedly abducted by aliens and you have a specific date, time, and place for their alledged abduction—and, of course, don't really care whether or not you ever obtain a verification of your information.

All humor aside, lots of things can be targeted using a coordinate system (sealed envelopes), or photographs illustrating ideas, concepts, plans, thoughts, words, and feelings.

Some good examples of things that should *not* be targeted are inaccessible areas like deep space, mythological beliefs or beings, aliens, or other unknowns that might be inaccessible; or for which there is not or cannot be feedback. An argument against this statement might be: well, you target nuclear-particles for physics and you can't see them. This is true. However, testing with accelerators and through other means can eventually verify what might have been postulated through the remote viewing. In other words, other forms of proof might eventually be proffered that verify the viewing information.

I'm not dead set against targeting things like the possible sites for downed UFOs, or crop circles, because in reality these events may not even be a direct result of UFOs or aliens; in which case verifiable information could be located, thus providing feedback. Such targets may also provide information that is testable in some way that provides further elucidation regarding their reality, even when they might be assumed as alien in origin. It's just that they should be targeted with extreme care and caution, and one should not make assumptions based on whatever information is provided. In other words, if these things are targeted, the targeting should be left to experts who have garnered sufficient experience with good remote viewing protocol to know the differences.

Targeting a remote viewer correctly in our time-space is difficult in the extreme. Unverifiable targeting in what might be seven or more dimensions, or beyond our known space/time, only exacerbates the situation. At this point, no one knows for certain if there is any truth at all to such hypotheses. Certainly I don't.

But, ideas, concepts, plans, thoughts, words, and feelings are fair game and can be targeted. There are a number of ways to do this, all of which are equally haphazard.

1. You can wait until the remote viewer brings up one of these subjects during actual targeting and then ask him or her to expand on it. There is a great risk that if there is no further information available, the remote viewer will invent the information because you have shown an interest. So, if you ask, don't accept the response until it's been obtained more than once over a period of time.

2. Ideas and concepts can be written out as questions and placed in sealed envelopes. The more care and thought that is put into trying to minimize the amount of viewing necessary to obtain an answer, the better off you will be, of course. Let's say you have a question about whether or not an idea will take hold; e.g., "Will body art increase in popularity?" Writing this question out takes a considerable amount of planning and thinking. For instance, there could be a substantial increase in tattooing, very little growth in body painting, but a whole new field could open up in decorative body jewelry implanted just below the skin. So, how you phrase the question is extremely important. A good rule of thumb is, the more abstract the idea, the more difficult it will be to provide appropriate targeting.

3. Thoughts and feelings are almost always going to be spontaneous. If you want this information over other types of detail, then you need to take particular care in how you frame your targeting. This is always a sealed envelope directive, or possibly a combination of protocols being used simultaneously. For instance, if you want to know what someone is thinking, you might place a photograph of that person in a sealed envelope, and then ask the viewer to describe what they perceive about the target. They will either produce a spontaneous statement about what the person is thinking, or they won't. You have to trust "intent" to drive them to the appropriate response. Telling viewers that you are interested in what a targeted person might be thinking, even when they don't know that person, generally won't work, because this forces the viewer into what's called a "forced-choice" scenario. There are only a handful of viewers in the world with sufficient experience to deal

with a forced-choice scenario, and all of them have more than twenty years of experience in remote viewing while operating under stringent protocols.

Strange or Unique Types of Protocols

Special protocols were developed over the years to address unique or strange requirements. Sometimes they were designed to answer very specific or narrow questions, such as "yes," "no," and "maybe." Sometimes they were designed to be used with other methods of psychic functioning, such as divining accurate locations, in conjunction with healing, sub-atomic or micro types of targets, or how to tag a specific event within a target when the exact time or date isn't known. There are even ways of increasing the probability of accuracy, although these are sometimes quite questionable.

Associative Remote Viewing

When you are faced with a forced-choice requirement, e.g., is it yes or is it no, is it white or black, do you go or not go, etc., then Associative Remote Viewing (ARV) is usually relied on to provide the answer.

As I said before, you cannot rely on the information remote viewers provide when asked to give a forced-choice responses. So the problem is multi-faceted:

First, in order for them to understand that a yes or no answer is required and nothing more, you have to tell them about the problem. This automatically front-loads the viewer with too much information. Too much information drives all the wrong things in the viewer's mind. What they "think" comes into play, instead of what they are "viewing." The viewer's likes and dislikes, preferences for outcome, and even a reluctance to deliver bad news alters the way they respond. So, you have to separate the viewer from the yes/no response in someway—thus the term "Associative" in ARV.

The way it works is identical to the Coordinate protocol, with the following change: First we must know what the specific forced-choice question is and the kind of answers it might require. For the sake of argument, lets assume that we want to know whether or not to invest in a stock we like for a period of thirty days. There are a number of steps we then take. We identify the specific period of interest: May 1 through 30. Then, instead of randomly choosing a single target from a pool of possible targets, two targets are chosen: Target A and Target B.

The same person who would normally determine what the target is does all of this. But remember no information is shared with the viewer, monitor, or Analyst.

Having chosen two targets, that person then assigns the values (the forced-choice) to each of the targets. In this case Target A becomes "invest," and Target B becomes "do not invest."

Let's assume for a moment that Target A is the picture of a mountain, and Target B is a bridge. Then:

Target A (Mountain)= Invest.

Target B (Bridge)= Do not invest.

All of this information is kept from all the other participants. The viewer is then asked to do a remote viewing one day prior to the day the decision must be made on whether or not to invest—let's assume April 30. The tasking is as follows:

"Please describe the picture you will be shown at 09:00 A.M. on June 1st." (NOTE: Assuming the investment period is May 1-30, then we will know for sure only on June the 1st whether or not an investment would have been a wise idea.)

The target is then described or drawn as accurately as possible by the viewer. The Analyst is then given the viewer's results, along with both pictures, and is asked to report which picture the viewer's comments or drawings most closely resembles. Let's assume the viewer comments on or draws a mountain.

This information is passed back to the person who selected the targets, who reports to the person wanting the information that; "You should invest in the stock."

But, at this point, we still do not actually know if the viewer was correct. We only know that the viewer's comments and drawings most closely matched the picture of the mountain, which equates to "invest," and so the stock is purchased.

Now, flash forward to June 1st. A review of how well the stock did is made on that date, and a decision is made *post-hoc* as to whether or not stock should have been purchased. If the stock did very well, then the person who determined the targets actually hands the viewer the picture of the mountain at 09:00 A.M. that morning. This would mean things worked really well. However, if on June 1st it's determined that the stock should not have been purchased, then the viewer should be given the picture of the bridge, in which case he sees that his viewing was not a good one and the remote viewing failed.

In no case should the viewer ever know what the other picture was, once he has been shown the one determined by the actual outcome. Since we do not know for sure how the viewer is actually getting his or her information regarding the target, there is a possibility this will interrupt or corrupt the process of information transfer.

There are ways of increasing the probability for success using ARV. These are:

1. By using more than one viewer. But please note that each viewer should have a different set of photographs representing the alternative choices. The reason for this is covered later in this book under handling of target materials and internal leakage.

2. By picking the specific time for actually doing the remote viewing. This is covered elsewhere in this book under the subject of Local Sidereal Time.

3. By making sure the pictures contain a very clear gestalt, which even the least effective viewers generally have no trouble with.

4. By making sure the dissimilarity between photographs is clearly evident.

5. By not altering the protocol in any way, and carrying it to completion—right or wrong.

But what if you can't decide between the pictures? Well, some have interpreted this to mean that no action should be taken. In the case of the stock investment this is meaningless, but in many yes or no, forced-choice questions, this could be very important. For instance, maybe you are trying to decide if you should buy property in the next week. An indefinite answer might mean to "wait."

Addressing Problems of Location

Contrary to general belief, remote viewing is seldom very good at locating things. Those who say it is should stop fantasizing and deluding themselves.

It can sometimes produce a very accurate picture of a specific location or event, but even in the rarest of cases, when it might be near perfect, it is still difficult locating that place or event on a map. For instance if someone looking for a kidnapped child produces a near perfect description of a trailer in a trailer park, the only problem remaining is placing that particular trailer inside one of the 1,285,000 trailer parks we have to select from.

But, now and then we may get lucky, and the viewing will contain other information of value. Maybe there is snow on the ground and it's early June, which definitely narrows the area in which that trailer park might be located. Or, perhaps the park our trailer is in is located adjacent to an amusement park that has a ride unique only to that park. But these kinds of results occur fewer times than might be expected.

What generates these false beliefs in accuracy is a combination of overselling the results the few times it actually worked well in locating something, and locating something through the use of logic while on a small search site, and misinterpreting this as remote viewing. In such a case, you might have been given a good general search area, lets say two by two miles, and lead information by a local police department. In which case, it may not be remote viewing at all, but good logical thinking combined with experience in thinking outside the box. (I know this implies that some police departments may have become routine or parochial in their approach, but sorry, people, it's true. You sometimes are.)

In attempting to find something paranormally, if you hope to use remote viewing, then you need to use something else as well—this is called dowsing.

Dowsing

Dowsing has been around at least as long as psychic functioning. Most have heard about this in connection with searching for water or minerals. The way we use dowsing with remote viewing is not much different.

There are numerous techniques used for dowsing, and since this is not a book on dowsing they won't be addressed here (except minimally). However, if you plan on using dowsing to locate something on a map, you probably want to do the remote viewing first. Remote viewing will produce a lot of information that is descriptive of the site; near edge of a lake, in hilly country, major power-lines nearby, some kind of flat roofed building with metal doors, etc. Once you've produced the remote viewing information just as you would for a coordinate or sealed envelope type of target, you then obtain a map of the area you think you might want to be searching in.

Usually this is accomplished in some sort of progressive way. If you are looking for a kidnapped victim who could be anywhere in America, then you obviously have to start with a map of America. Once you've dowsed an area, then you need to obtain a map of that area. As an example, if it's central Virginia, then you need a map of central Virginia. You then isolate the location to a specific county and obtain a map of that county. You can further isolate a specific area within that county, and obtain a map for that area, etc., until you have narrowed it to the point of looking for features that match from your remote viewing. You do the remote viewing first, so that looking at the map details does not front-load you on what to expect. Don't expect to be right on the money the first time you try. I once looked for nearly three years before I found a person I was looking for, and never did succeed through dowsing.

There are cases where dowsing was used by the military with a great deal of accuracy. This necessity of locating things led to two or three of the viewers being formally trained in dowsing.

I was originally trained in dowsing while assigned to the STARGATE unit at Fort Meade. I was later trained formally, at the Cognitive Sciences Laboratory at SRI-International, by an internationally-known dowser with decades of experience. The differences were notable. You always get what you are willing to pay for.

Note that the use of dowsing does not preclude following established protocols for remote viewing. People sometimes fail to remember that when they begin combining methodologies.

Using Remote Viewing for Healing
Until recently I would have stated that I had not yet seen any examples of remote healing. But, in the past year there

have been some very intriguing experiments done in just this area. Early findings still do not prove if healing is or is not taking place, but there is a marked improvement in quality of life that cannot be ignored.

Be that as it may, and contrary to what some are saying, remote viewing is not remote healing. They are two completely different animals. Remote viewing has been and can be used in the art of healing, however, usually as an addition to some other diagnostic tool. One must understand that the times when this might be of value are extremely rare, especially since remote viewing should *absolutely never be used* in place of normal diagnostic tools.

It is used the same as any coordinate or sealed envelope target, only you would include something identifying the patient as the target. No information would be given to the viewer except the sealed envelope and a statement such as, "Describe what I need to know to heal the person identified within the envelope."

By not providing any other information, you can use things like gender, age, race, and overall health as sort of a check and balance system for the information you are looking for. If the viewer gets all of those items right, then what s/he says about the patient's health might also be more true than not. In any event, the remote viewing information can be used to more specifically target other diagnostic tools or medical laboratory investigations to pinpoint a patient's illness. In no case should it be used to direct a medical procedure. It isn't that accurate, and it certainly isn't that dependable.

Ways of targeting patients that have been successfully tested in the past are by placing a small piece of a patient's X-ray in an envelope with the patient's identifying number, targeting a patient's lab results, or asking the viewer to describe what might be emotionally disturbing a patient. All of these might provide indications of where to go next in diagnosing a patient's problem, or which diagnostic tool will prove most profitable.

Sub-Atomic or Micro Structures

Again, using the coordinate or sealed envelope protocol is the normal route here. However the difficulty then becomes how to frame the question, as we can only hypothesize as to how most sub-atomic structures look, and there are very few ways to actually display them. One might deal with this in the way they are specified within the targeting envelope. Some examples:

Normal phrase in envelope: "Describe the wave function for target identified within the envelope."

Suggested: "Describe the wave function for target identified within the envelope as compared to the wave function of an Alpha particle." (Or whatever one might assume to be closely related or similar.) In the case where something has never even been hypothesized, you might say: "Describe this particle in a way that will permit the development of a hypothesis for testing."

Micro type targets can be just as tough. If you are looking for something like the key to a DNA strand, or the primary receptor for the AIDS virus cell, such targets almost always rely on the viewers' ability to communicate what they are perceiving in a way that the receiver of the information can understand and visualize. For this reason, the following is strongly recommended when attempting to tackle such targets:

1. Use only very experienced remote viewers with established and very well tested track records. While this appears simple, it isn't. Just because a viewer claims to have a track record doesn't mean it's real.

2. Use viewers that are talented in the visual arts. There seems to be a direct link between someone's ability to clearly visualize and their ability to correctly pass along information they perceive.

3. Have the viewer attempt to produce remote viewing

information on the same target two or three times but do not let them know that they are doing so. Familiarity with the problem seems to bring a better success rate with micro types of targets, even when the familiarity is developed through psychic means alone. (Note: This does not preclude the monitor or anyone else in the room with the viewer from being kept totally blind as to the target as well. No one in the room should know that it is the same target.)

4. Viewers should be encouraged to use whatever visual method is necessary to present the best possible picture of what it is they might perceive. This would include all art forms and mediums of expression: clay, drawing, or even construction from wood, metals, and plastics, pre-formed or otherwise.

Event Related Targets

One of the hardest types of targets is an event for which the actual event time or date has not been well-established. Many feel that some hint as to what the actual event might be needs to be passed along to the viewer. This is absolutely *not* what you want to do. There are a number of reasons why.

First is the assumption that the event even took place. Since a date and time cannot be well-established, that automatically makes the rest of the information suspect. One cannot assume that an event occurred when there is nothing more substantial to go on than rumor.

As an example, let us use what is presumed to be the effects of a huge explosion over an isolated area of frozen tundra in the northern territories of Siberia. We know it probably occurred sometime within a given 30-day period of a specific date, because of all the rumors coming out of the region, carried by hunters and woodsmen; but aside from this we have no other idea about what happened. So, we actually travel there and talk with people living in the area. They have vague recollections of a huge bang followed by strange lights in the sky that night. We actually see on the ground that there are shattered trees three feet in diameter, and they lay outward in what appears to be a blast effect radius from a center or core location. There might even be fire damage.

One might conclude from this evidence that there has been an explosion. We want to use a remote viewer to actually pinpoint the specific date and, if possible, a time for this explosion. We can do this by narrowing the event down to the approximate 72-hour window we've developed from talks with the locals. How do you go about it?

First, it is a huge assumption that an explosion took place at all. There may be nothing else in our memory banks that could account for the strangeness of the event, but this does not mean one should assume that it is an explosion. There are lots of things it could be, and remote viewing is the best way to open to those possibilities. So, to begin with, we simply target the viewer on "center of mass," or the core of the event location. We can do that by providing specific coordinates placed within a sealed envelope.

Now we already possess some very interesting details concerning the event, but what would be nice would be a description of the event itself and a more accurate time at which it occurred. That way, other data we might want to investigate can be brought into play—e.g., perhaps studying the chemical make-up within the rings of surrounding trees on the outskirts of the blast area, or looking at mineral deposits on ice in the surrounding mountains, etc.

We accomplish this by giving the monitor working with the viewer the following guidelines:

"Ask the viewer to provide us with a general description of the location within the envelope. If the viewer indicates that a major event has occurred, then walk them backward in four-hour increments. If no event has occurred, then walk them forward in four-hour increments."

The question inside the envelope should read: "Describe the event that occurred before or after 12:00 Noon (and pick the middle date).

Why would we want to do it this way? We know that as soon as you start moving viewers around in time, they know there is an event they should be looking for. Since they were asked to describe what's identified as a location first, then if they describe the location correctly but not the event, we know they are being accurate but have to move forward in time. If they describe the location and appear to be reporting on the effects from the event, then we know they have to be moved backward in time. In both cases they have already demonstrated their accuracy by giving accurate descriptions of the location. If they do not describe the location accurately, we know we don't even have to read the rest of their remote viewing information because they weren't at the right target. In both cases, we've allowed the viewer to be accurate in a double blind fashion first. If you need better accuracy than four hours, you can re-target later using the same method, moving forward or backward in 30 minute epochs. Once a time has been well established, you can then re-target to get more detail about the event itself—which could have been almost anything.

Just for interest sake, I've been using the event at the Tunguska Basin, June 30, 1908 as an example. The event site gives the appearance that a huge explosion occurred which leveled trees for a twenty-mile radius. It reportedly knocked farm animals off their feet nearly 400 kilometers away. It has been variously attributed to a meteorite, black hole, and anti-matter. I would suggest based on remote viewing, that it was actually a fairly large meteorite traveling at a high rate of speed (probably in excess of 60k feet per second), that struck the outer atmosphere layers nearly perpendicular to the bow wave of the earth, dissolving in a single focused cone of energy over the Tunguska Basin, creating damage like a shaped charge would do on the exterior of armor plating. But, this is only conjecture and has not been further verified. [RV Sept. 16, 1988].

Basic Methodologies and Styles Used by Remote Viewers for Collecting and Processing Information

Up until now, I've been talking about *protocols* and things that effect them. Now I will talk about *methods* that remote viewers use to disassociate from the here and now, in order to collect psychic information.

Within public forums and on the Internet, there's been a lot of ugly talk in the past about which "method" is genuinely associated with remote viewing and which isn't. This is kind of humorous to me, as anyone arguing this is missing the entire point. Since protocols are scientifically developed and tested with some rigor, any changes require substantial testing and evaluating before they can be considered acceptable. Methods, on the other hand, or how a psychic collects information, do not have to be tested or evaluated. As long as they are performed within the boundaries of acceptable protocols, it is unnecessary.

So, now I will talk about a few of these. The full list is actually pretty long, so I will stick with the most significant of them.

Extended Remote Viewing (ERV)

This is the name given to some to the original remote viewing methodologies used by remote viewers at Fort Meade. It is accurate only in that it designates a time period—approximately September 1978 through September 1984. It is also accurate in that it describes nearly all remote viewers' approaches to remote viewing as some form of

self-induced altered state. It is inaccurate, in that no two
viewers ever operated the same, were ever in the same
altered state, nor produced information through the same
method of internalized processing.

Some would point to that and say: "See, precisely what
was wrong with the program. No consistency." However,
they would be totally wrong, as this was a period of time
in which some of the best remote viewing ever produced
by the project was generated. It was also one of the most
prolific periods of remote viewing output.

Almost without exception, the targets were always
contained within sealed envelopes, and the viewers were
allowed to offer what is now considered "free response"
regarding the target of interest.

Viewers accomplished this by developing their own
means of focus or meditation, which in turn induced a very
effective self-imposed altered state. This altered state
allowed total disassociation from the immediate surroundings and free association with the target's surroundings
and events, which were then reported on.

The surviving remote viewers of the time would tell you
that this apparent free form, though viewed by many as
difficult to deal with, was effective in the extreme. The
people who generally didn't like this methodology were of
course not the people who were required to produce the
information, nor were they the ones who were required to
analyze it. They were the people who had to "sell the idea"
of remote viewing to others. Those who observe someone
using this methodology, if they do not have an open mind
to paranormal functioning in the first place, will almost
always feel uncomfortable. In shorter terms, it was objec-
tionable to everyone but the viewer.

Learning the methodology is simple. Through meditation,
or other devices, training, etc., you learn to put yourself into
a semi-trance state, or disassociate with your immediate
surroundings, while maintaining a focus on your end goal,

which is to establish an association with whatever the target might be. Then you report on what you might be seeing, feeling, hearing, or otherwise perceiving. The ability to learn this requires a considerable focus and lots of practice, which must all be done within protocol. It is not a cheap way to learn remote viewing, since it is time and labor intensive.

Controlled Remote Viewing (Sometimes Referred to as Coordinate Remote Viewing [CRV])

Originally developed by Ingo Swann while working at SRI-International, this is now the most commonly referred to or generally accepted method of remote viewing, primarily because of the perceived ease of training, and the numbers of people who claim expertise in teaching it. However, what most people do not understand is, how it is taught and how it is actually used for general applications follow two completely different sets of rules. Those who are trained in it are not automatically vaccinated with all the knowledge they need to apply it properly. Something as simple as following an appropriate protocol in setting up the target, as in protocols for proper target handling, is little understood or even unknown to many.

The originator of this training system did not distribute an all-inclusive document with this training system either. If you truly understand the training system and the rigorous basis upon which it was developed, then you can understand why. It was never intended for wholesale use within the general population. There are no details, therefore, on how or why something is done in training, and then never done within an application, or vice versa.

There is an extant copy of a document available over the Internet that is alleged to be a complete CRV manual, but because it is designed to address training, it does not address any of the issues regarding applications. But already there are many who are using it as a guide for applications as well as training, introducing further error into the system.

The premise behind CRV is that all human beings receive and deal with psychic information on a day-to-day basis. The problem is, in order to recognize psychic information and willfully use it, it has to bubble up to cognition, where we can attempt to control it. This automatically allows false data to be introduced by the conscious mind, which introduces error through fantasy, lack of control, emotional reactions to the base information, etc. Or, at least, that is the assumption.

The rather draconian CRV training system is designed to teach the unconscious mind to deliver commands to the system without going through the cognition process. In other words, if the target's a mountain, then let the hand be commanded to draw a mountain by the subconscious without cognitive interference.

There probably is merit to this theory, in that one can readily demonstrate that a structured or ordered learning system can be used to entrain the subconscious to respond based on psychic input. But, only under the strictest controls of protocol and only after a long and rigorous training period which takes place outside the protocol controlling process. A point largely missed by many.

Testing of individuals who have been formally trained with CRV sometimes shows phenomenal responses in training scenarios outside protocols. But these same people fail miserably when forced to operate within protocols. Why? Probably because the person doing the training thoroughly understands the training process, but does not understand the basic or underlying theory behind it. Nor do the trainers take into account that students' actual talent level plays a great deal in how well they will do with any methodology in the first place. The trainers have come to put too much faith in a process, which is little understood from the outset.

In my opinion, the CRV process was originally designed to produce almost robotic-like responses from an individual, which could be structured to fall into basic categories or differing degrees of information and complexity. These differing degrees or stages are stacked in a linear fashion, and through rigorous training the student works his or her way down through them over and over again, until they are able to automatically respond within specific categories without thinking. It takes an enormous degree of personal discipline to successfully negotiate the CRV training program, after which the cognitive thought process is supposed to have been minimized within the remote viewing process.

It actually does eventually instill a very controlled response structure on the person desiring to be a remote viewer. But, in most cases they still walk away with very little understanding for the appropriate protocols and why they are necessary. For most people it over-simplifies a very complex issue that no one truly understands in the first place. But does it work?

The true answer is, yes. It works just about as well as any other training or remote viewing methodology invented over the years. No better or no worse. Ultimately, it is still driven by the natural or innate talent of the student and not the teacher.

Tarot Cards, Channeling, Automatic Writing, Scrying, or Other Exotic Forms of Information Production

There is a lot of controversy surrounding these issues. I feel a need to address them here. This would be a major issue if methodology meant the same thing as protocol, but it doesn't. As I've tried to differentiate between methods and protocol, one is an absolute, and one isn't.

In a number of cases, valuable information has been derived from the reading of tarot cards, channeled materials, automatic writing, or scrying. One only has to look at history to find many references to these occurrences. For advocates of one method of producing psychic information to bad-mouth another is like the pot calling the kettle black. The primary problem lies in the fact that these other methods have not traditionally followed the approved protocols that are used for remote viewing. The psychics or others within the room are seldom blind to the target, there is no effort to control the data once collected, and a lot of the reporting is done in hindsight, without the record keeping that is usually found with remote viewing. This does not mean the methods don't work.

In my observation, over twenty-one years, some very good psychic data has been provided by card readers, channelers, automatic writers, and even the momentarily focused skeptic *while operating within an appropriate remote viewing protocol.* In my experience, it is just about as accurate as information I've seen produced under ERV or CRV as well. The point here is that the appropriate protocol seems to put all the right puzzle pieces in the right place to allow psychic functioning to take place.

If the target is appropriately set up, the intent of the participants is dealt with properly, an expectation for success is underscored, and all known leakage paths are shut down, there will be psychic information production. If the protocol is an acceptable remote viewing protocol, then, whether the information produced is by looking at a symbol on a deck of cards and psychically interpreting it, or it is produced through the rigors of CRV is not material. The base requirements have been met from a scientific standpoint, so the question is moot.

Many people have heard me say that if someone would like to stand on their head in a bucket of pea soup while whistling Dixie through their left nostril and can produce information within the remote viewing protocol, then I'm willing to call it remote viewing.

It is true that the greater the methodological requirements you bring into play between yourself and the target, the tougher it is to produce the psychic information. I will be the very first to readily admit there is a huge possibility for distraction in standing on one's head in a bucket of soup. The idea would be to reduce the distraction, not add to it.

But, that rule is not only applicable to someone who is upside down in a bucket of soup. It is applicable across the board, to all methodologies.

So once again, I find myself stating that it is more than likely a difference in individual psychic talent and the proclivities that support it that gives best expression to successful psychic functioning within a commonly acceptable protocol.

My observations over many years, leads me to believe that the simpler you can keep the process, the better. The more natural talent you can bring into the room, the better. The fewer conditions you require, or variables you apply, the better.

Chapter Seven

— ✸ —

Training and Learning

I don't think it's possible to train someone to be psychic. That's like saying you can train someone to smell better. Few of us pay much attention to what passes through our nostrils, till it's strongly repugnant, or excessively appealing. Otherwise, a smell wafts in and out through our nose and we pretty much don't pay any attention to it.

Combat soldiers pay attention to smell. Ask any combat veteran what the odor of turbine fuel washing out of a helicopter engine, or the smell of blood rotting in the sun, or maybe gun oil, does to them. They learned to differentiate very quickly between the smell of the food they eat and what the enemy eats. I know guys who could step out on a trail under a triple-canopy jungle and tell you how long ago someone had passed, their nationality, whether they were men or women, and healthy or unhealthy, just by the residual body odors clinging to the still air.

Are we ever formally taught to smell? Clearly the answer is no. However, we can learn to pay attention to the differences. That happens through experience. If you don't experience the odor of jet fuel and equate it to something meaningful, then jet fuel is never going to make any difference to you.

People who suddenly discover they are psychic, begin to

do this automatically. You help people discover their psychic nature by helping them to have their first psychic experience. If they are open-minded enough, they discover that it is part of their own nature, and they almost automatically begin to listen to their inner voice. They attempt to differentiate between the noise and what might be valid input. Standing outside of someone's head and dictating what is noise and what isn't, is impractical in theory and impossible in action. Like the soldier, someone wanting to capitalize on their psychic abilities in a big way simply needs to practice paying attention. Since no two people pay attention the same way or process information in exactly the same way, probably no one way is best for doing this. In other words, there is *no magic method for turning someone into a gifted psychic.* If you believe there is, you are already coming out of the starting gate backward.

This means you are more than likely to garner just about the same amount of "learning" from any one training program as from another. Your ability to pay attention and deal with your innermost processing rests totally on your own shoulders. This should be a loud warning about how much you believe about training systems.

Nevertheless I would like to provide some guidelines about what you should be able to expect or not expect from a valid training program, some ideas about what might be going on during any form of training, and the major differences I've noticed between training scenarios and actual applications.

What's Going on During Training

It has long been clear to me that no one learns anything new during any kind of training program. Actually an "unlearning" is taking place, a systematic and detailed destruction of old concepts and automated systems that have been installed since the day we were born. As we pass through life, we pick up beliefs like Velcro, none of which are based on fundamental truth.

We begin our instruction with parents who, while sincerely motivated, instill in us what they believe is true, whether it actually is or not. We are taught by teachers who attempt to pass on knowledge to us, at least as they understand it to be. Whether it is bound within their own idealism and rhetoric, or the fact that they themselves might have been duped or not, isn't material.

Then we have our religious ministers who are, like it or not, bound tightly within closed loops of spiritual perceptions or parochial rules they dare not exceed for fear of eternal condemnation.

And then we have our peer groups, which are almost always consumed with a concern for overall image, reputation, or the outside perceptions of others.

Other mentors, like radio, magazines, television, government, and newspapers produce effects that can have even greater subtlety.

Habits we form rule the way we actually process information. We live in an age that essentially requires us to process ever expanding amounts of information day-to-day, hour-to-hour, and moment-to-moment. We don't have time to give to things the kinds of focus and considered thought that we should. At least, that is the excuse. In reality we do, but most simply have forgotten how.

When we are faced with a problem, we rapidly collect what information we can. As the information begins to come in (some of it psychic, by the way), we rapidly accept what seems to fit and discard what seems not to. Eventually, enough information is processed to provide a needed conclusion. We take action on the conclusion, delete the information that wasn't apparently supportive, and file only the material that supported our action, then move on to the next processing requirement. When you overload a system that operates like this, you quickly learn that it is driven by two things:

1. Rapid information processing (minimizing input).

2. Rapid solution finding (quick conclusions).

As we are inundated with more and more processing requirements, the amount of information we collect to address any specific problem begins to become less and less, and our conclusions start coming quicker and quicker.

Jumping to conclusions without obtaining considerable input in my opinion thwarts the psychic process. Note: I did not say processing. Rapid processing or no processing is actually desired, because it has a tendency to prevent conscious manipulation of the data. Therefore, an appropriate goal would be to expand the amount of information you are letting in, while delaying the necessity for conclusion, but retaining the speed of processing. Which is somewhat the reverse of what is commonly accepted.

Observed Differences Between Men and Women

First I would like to make it abundantly clear that any comments, statements, or rumors you might have heard about any differences in quality, ability, or accuracy between women and men are fabrications. They are simply not true. However, over the years I've observed lots of interesting differences between the two genders. If for nothing else, these differences should be of value to researchers and scientists. Observed differences between men and women while remote viewing are not differences of quality or quantity, but in technique or approach.

During viewing women are more apt to describe the target verbally than through drawing. Men are just the opposite. In fact, sometimes you can get almost perfect drawings of targets from men, but their verbalization will be totally wrong; and vice versa for women. Experience will usually smooth out the degrees of variances somewhat, but this will hold true in many cases. That's why you have to be willing to let women and men do their own thing with regard to methods. Some women will feel a need to "channel" the information. Some men will feel a need to "construct" it. What's more interesting is how people deal with these issues.

If a man is attempting to do a remote viewing of a target and says; "I need clay to model this in," that's cool. He gets clay. If a woman says, "Wait a minute. I need to check with my guides," and opens a channel to her guides, she's almost automatically considered to be a raving loon. Throwing clay on a table—okay. Throwing bones from a jar—not okay.

I read an article once that talked about the differences in white matter and gray matter inside the human skull. Men and women have different amounts of each, one more than the other; but, the article said since men have much larger brain mass than women, they still possess the equivalent of whatever matter the women have the most of. This article, exposing the differences between men and women's capacity to deal with spatial perception, concluded that women would generally have more trouble dealing with spatial problems than men do. I'm not sure I buy that. Sure, men might be able to draw a map more effectively, but what's that got to do with figuring out how to get from point A to B? If these differences were meaningful, then we wouldn't have women piloting high-speed jets, driving racecars, or operating complex remote-machinery. It just means they do it differently. Where we learn to respect and employ the differences in perception or spatial ability, we can actually benefit to a much greater degree.

Another area in which men and women are different is emotionally. Women sometimes seem to be in closer connection to their emotions than men are. This certainly is true in my observations of remote viewers. Women are quicker to point out emotion-generating events within the remote viewing. Men are less inclined to talk about them. This presents a major difference in processing that needs to be addressed up front when dealing with remote viewing information. What is interesting is there is sometimes a belief that reporting on emotions or permitting them during remote viewing is either a sign of weakness or instability. This is wrong! Emotional weakness is not being open about what you are feeling, and thinking that you are being somehow judged because of it. Instability, on the other hand, can be indicated through emotion, but it is not the emotion itself but the person's inability to differentiate between his or her own emotion and that being generated by a target that should be questioned.

For the most part, differences between men and women have to do with internal balance, where they are centered. Imagine this as represented by a balancing scale. Most men have generally more male characteristics than female, and women more female than male. However, it is possible for men and women to be nearly equal in some cases, at least as pertains to characteristics. While there is no data to support it, I believe those who are closest to the center generally make the best remote viewers. This simply means they may be well-equipped to handle psychic input with fewer major internalized processing changes required.

Interestingly, where I have observed a severe unbalance of male and female characteristics or attributes, I've sometimes observed a high degree of instability in remote viewing. Formal testing may one day prove this observation to be correct or itself out-of-balance.

Differences Between Learning and Applications

One thing that most people do not recognize, especially those not familiar with remote viewing, is the difference between learning remote viewing and applying it. In the beginning, there was very little difference the same protocols applied in applications and in learning. But over time, a lot of the developments in training essentially sidestepped rules of protocol. There aren't many differences but they are critically important, and can determine if you are actually remote viewing or deluding yourself.

First, let me say that if I were teaching someone to remote view, I would be forcing the use of strict and unforgiving protocols at the outset. Please note: I said "protocols" and not "methods." Protocols are the rules you will have to eventually comply with anyway, so there is no easy way to introduce them. You simply start with the minimum acceptable practice from the outset. I chose not to teach remote viewing but others do, so I will share with you some warnings.

Most of the training systems in use today do not recognize the necessity for keeping everyone in proximity to the remote viewing totally blind to the target. The argument usually made is something like, "How can we reinforce a correct response and not encourage an incorrect response, if we don't know what the target is?"

Not following the protocols during training, for any reason, leaves the door wide open to a result which is not necessarily being produced through psychic means. The student may have gotten the information through psychic means, but then again, may have gotten it through any one of a number of other ways.

Remote viewing protocol requires the remote viewer be blind, or have no other form of access to the target they are being asked to provide information on. This means no hints, no front-loading, no bending of the rules. In many, if not most, training programs, someone in the room, whether it is the monitor or not, usually knows what the specific target is. A sensitive person can then do what is called a cold reading: provide information by "reading" the non-verbal feedback they get from the person who knows what is real or not real about the target. A lot of people will tell you this isn't possible unless you are highly trained, and I will tell you that's hogwash.

When you were young, how many times did it seem to you that your parents were psychic and knew what you were going to do even before you did it? When's the last time your boss cut you off before you embarrassed yourself? How many times did you think, "*Wow, what a gorgeous babe,*" only to have her suddenly come on to you? None of this was psychic functioning, it was reading body language. We all do it. It's one of the reasons movies are so interesting. We aren't just listening to the dialog when we go to the movies, we go to see the visuals, the background. Even the music in the background is helping to deliver the visual message. If you don't believe that, then turn down the volume the next time you are watching a good movie on TV, and see if you lose interest in it. I recently watched an entire American movie in Hungarian on Hungarian National television. I didn't get all the meaning, but I'll bet I understood it enough to comment intelligently on its contents. Of course I don't speak Hungarian.

The point is if you want psychic information, you have to eliminate all other forms or possibilities of information transfer. These are commonly referred to as "paths of leakage" or "leakage paths." True, we could train to increase our other sensitivities and this will be effective in how we deal with problems, and that's nice, but it isn't remote viewing. Calling it that does a clear disservice to both.

So, we need to identify violations of protocols within a training schema and eliminate them. In the case of most training programs extant, that means no one knowing the target while you are attempting to collect information on it.

Another form of leakage deals with information handling and protection. I will be the last one to imply that anyone is cheating. In most cases, people do not cheat—at least consciously. However, in rare cases I have seen people innocently add information after the termination of a remote viewing effort—it was something they forgot to add during the session, or something they remembered they were thinking at the time. (Note: When this happens it should always be noted immediately and the remote viewing abandoned, discarded, and labeled as a blown protocol.)

This kind of reaction almost never happens in applications, but it should. This is especially true when someone is using applications to prove the efficacy of remote viewing to the public. The reason why is simple. It is a violation of protocol.

There are numerous occasions when a remote viewer will add that last little something to the information, as it is being logged or filed. The problem is, this might be after someone has seen it that might know what the target is. Just a raised eyebrow can generate a need to expound on something one way or another. In some cases, this could result in an accusation of fraud, even though it might not have been done intentionally, it's best to discard the information.

The problem is that the care taken in control of the information during training and during applications is usually totally different. During applications, if handled correctly, materials are religiously controlled and properly maintained. No one wants to negate whatever effort has gone into the actual information collection.

In training, this is usually not the case. Controls, if they exist at all, are minimized. This sometimes provides an opportunity for viewers to accidentally see each other's work; they might sometimes see each other's targets, or make comparisons and then talk a great deal about what is going on. There just isn't any guarantee that it isn't happening.

The problem this creates is that if it is done during training, the proper habits and exercises are not the only things being reinforced. The negative ones are being reinforced as well. It is always a lot easier to break protocol, unconsciously or accidentally, when appropriate habits are not being reinforced.

Habits go a long way toward insuring how the materials are being handled, logged, controlled, and filed, or who ultimately has access and why. Some people file training materials with applications materials, which further degrades the relationship between them. Bad habits contribute to the development of leakage paths. The smart person understands that when it comes to remote viewing their practices have got to be sound and beyond reproach from the outset.

Selection of Targets for Training

For obvious reasons, targets are not specifically chosen for applications. But for training or research purposes they can be. A considerable amount is known about how targets affect a remote viewer. For many reasons, great care should go into choosing which kinds of targets are used and in which combinations. Targets used for training (as well as research) should generally comply with the following guidelines.

Early Stages of Training

a. Training targets should stand alone, and be well-defined from their surroundings or other objects or possible targets in their proximity.

It is not a good idea to select buildings, objects, or things that are crowded in with other significant buildings, objects, or things. For example, don't select a single statue in a garden of statues, or a unique structure standing next to another unique structure.

b. Targets should not be too complex.

From an instructional as well as a research viewpoint, targets that are too complex are almost impossible to evaluate. Inevitably, if someone talks a great deal or draws numerous details, some of them will match something on the target. It is very difficult for most new viewers to separate details from major gestalts. It also compounds the evaluation problems of the researcher when trying to determine how to match the results to a stack of decoys (decoys are randomly selected pictures that are used for controls in experiments). It might seem that Niagra Falls would make a great target, but depending on where the outbounder might be standing, or how the targeting is set up, you could get reams of information that will all be pertinent in some way to the target. A better target would be the observation tower on the Canadian side of the falls.

c. Training targets should contain major gestalts.

Major features unique to the specific target should be present. As an example, a water-park with a long slide or a unique archway entry with a repetitive pattern would be desirable. These will produce a significant response in viewers, where items or features that are common to most sites will not. Remember, you are expecting new remote viewers to acclimate to a new system of cognition. This is difficult in the best of conditions. Targets with unique features increase the probability that they will notice them.

d. Limit the list of major gestalts.

This has to do with complexity as well. If there are too many variants within the target pool, the viewer essentially gets lost while trying to identify them. Major gestalts that seem to go a long way in training someone are: land water interfaces, varying degrees of rugged terrain, sparse to heavy influence of structures within the target, the type of terrain; desert, tundra, etc., predominant color, people, and activity. These alone provide for a wealth of possibility while instructing a new remote viewer. As an example, a target photograph could contain a mountain, hills, flat plain, valleys, or ravines. Each brings its own gestalt to the overall response.

Later Stages of Training

Variety is the spice of life. Once viewers begin to understand where the information is coming from (inside the head) it is time to begin to provide them with a greater variety of targets. What I'm talking about here does not require changing the original target pool. As viewers hone their skills, they will begin to provide more details about the content of the target. The increase in variety comes from changing the focus of what you are interested in them producing. In other words, it is no longer a question of producing a major gestalt about the target, you must let them know that you are interested in more details. If they say there is a building, what kind is it? If they describe hills, what about them? What's there, trees, grass, orchards, roads, a farm? They need to know they are expected to more accurately refine their responses beyond the major gestalts.

Only when the viewer has demonstrated that they can do this should any attempt be made to begin targeting things that violate the original a. through d. list above. It's only when they have demonstrated they can tell the differences that they should be burdened with picking a specific structure out of a group of structures.

What the Viewer Sees

It is unfortunate that the term remote viewing was originally selected to define this protocol of information production. It is constantly being misinterpreted to mean actually "seeing" the target. This is further complicated by a few who talk about being out-of-body when they are participating in a remote viewing. Since it's not possible to confirm out-of-body travel versus garden variety psychic functioning, it is impossible to know if someone is actually seeing the target. I can say that this is generally not the case. If someone does actually "see" something, it is almost always a close approximation or a close representation of reality, but not reality itself.

Putting out-of-body events to the side for a moment, if you believe you are actually seeing a target, you may assume that you can take your time in looking it over. Nothing could be further from the truth.

In actuality, when remote viewers open to a target or attempt to collect information on it, they are doing something akin to a quick taste. As in using our sense of taste, it is a sensation that strikes home very quickly. There is good in that, but also bad.

If, for instance, when you are blindfolded and someone puts a small bit of strawberry on your tongue, as soon as you rub it across your palate you know it's strawberry— not much processing going on there. But, if someone puts a small piece of something else on your tongue, which has been soaked in strawberry syrup, you are in trouble when it comes to identifying what it might be. Remote viewing is much the same way.

If you are overwhelmed by something in the target, e.g., a strawberry flavor, it is nearly impossible to dig out the details hidden by it. It can be done, but only if one doesn't jump to conclusions about strawberries. The same holds true for the opposite. If that's all it is, a small bit of strawberry, then it's nearly impossible to tell when to stop trying to perceive what might be there in addition to it, when there is really nothing else there. One prevents the flow of information, and the other encourages invention of information, all the while encouraging us to believe we are still in full contact with the original target, which we definitely are not. When a viewer tastes the target, it is only for a few nanoseconds and then contact is broken. The rest of the exercise is internalized processing, or determining when strawberry is important and when it is not. It is definitely not a full-scale model or pictogram laid out in total wonderment before our mind's eye.

Sometimes this happens, but only on the rarest of occasions, and always for very specific and/or limited reasons, which further complicates the process.

Additional confusion enters regarding visualization, when viewers are told to expect specific kinds of information based on their degree of talent, their current stage of training, ability, expertise, or experience, when none of that applies or has any real meaning.

Unfortunately, anything can happen on day one or in your twentieth year of experience. This is important to know, because it is currently implied in the literature and in books, or in talks by those who really don't know, that this is what you should be striving for; and, it is mythological. I will tell you in full honesty that if this is what you expect and what you are striving for, you are wasting your time and eventually you will be sadly disappointed.

Information comes in many ways to the viewer, and if not primarily through vision then through what? Well, this is difficult to explain. You will have perceptions about the target that are as vague as a movement you caught with the corner of your eye, the faint hint of an aroma, or a feeling that puts goose bumps on the backs of your arms. It is almost never direct but needs to be interpreted in some way.

Many teaching programs out there claim to take most of this "interpretation" out of the process of remote viewing. If you buy into that, good luck. Humans are cognitive beings, and nothing reaches our waking mind that has not been processed. You may temporarily fool yourself into thinking you aren't thinking, you may bury the processing to a point that you actually don't think you are really processing, but you are. Critics of my position on this state that I don't have a full understanding of what is going on in such a case, that the mind can be trained to "automatically respond" to certain stimuli, without processing.

They are certainly right, but only when the mind is put through a long sequence in forced choice training. And as soon as you begin to overlay the mind with forced choice, you are simply reversing the system. You are putting the processing at the fore instead of the end, reducing the breadth of the response parameters, and eliminating unconscious spontaneity. The unconscious spontaneous result accounts for more accuracy and detail in remote viewing than any other form of response.

The best approach is to attempt to understand "how" you process information. Study how your mind works. Do you have a proclivity to envision backyard swimming pools whenever an in-ground fluid reservoir is part of a target? Do you feel cool to the touch when there is fear involved with a target? Does your nose itch when there is smoke? You should study your subtle body-mind responses and try to establish an understanding of what you do when you are subjected to something real within a target. You should develop an understanding for the language your subconscious uses to communicate with your conscious mind. The language is dynamic, it changes frequently, and it will surprise you at times, but that is where you will find accuracy in your perceptions. In the old days, it was called going with your gut.

Good Practices

A number of things that initially seem more difficult, in the long run assist in developing your remote viewing talent. These are what I consider good practices. I've listed the ones that I feel are probably the most important. (Note: These are applicable to the learning process and are somewhat modified when it comes to applications.)

1. Always do your remote viewing totally blind to the target—no hints, no front-loading, no one in the room with you who knows what the target is, and no other possibility of information transfer other than through psychic means.

2. Always keep your own notebook about what you are thinking and why you are thinking it, with the goal of learning something about your method of internal cognitive processing.

3. Initially try and stick with major gestalts, slowly working your way into more detail. Open to whatever your subconscious wants to share with you, when it wants to share it.

4. Retain your sense of humor. Your subconscious is a trickster, a joker. It will play with you. Enjoy the ride. This is important. When it can deliver information no other way, it will deliver it buried in the humor.

5. Understand that you are embarking on a learning process that never stops. Since your own personal language of the mind is a dynamic one, you will never cease having to learn or understand something about it. It is a never-ending process. If you think you can get away with a few weeks effort and then know it all, you need to take up bowling or something less stressful.

Bad Practices

I could probably write an entire book on this, but it really isn't necessary. Almost without exception, if you feel like you are fooling yourself, it's a bad practice. If you feel like you are not doing the right thing, it's a bad practice. If you feel like someone is pulling your leg, they probably are. But, just for clarity's sake, I will list some of the worst of the lot.

1. Don't make lists of things that have to "be" in order for it to work. All you are really doing is making a list of reasons for failure. Learn to operate regardless of the place, time, or circumstance. You don't learn to taste, smell, hear, see, or touch within narrow parameters, so why try and force yourself to "perceive" only under certain conditions.

2. Except for the formalities of protocols that should not be violated in any way, take whatever anyone says to you with a grain of salt. That goes for what you are reading here. No one has all the answers. Everyone is learning as they go. In fact, the way to judge if someone really knows what they are doing will be their willingness to admit this.

3. While learning, never, never, never accept hints about the target, accept any form of front-loading, or permit someone who knows what the target is to be in your presence while you are remote viewing. This is important for a number of reasons, not the least of which is—if there is any room for doubt in your mind, this will produce it, and you will never know for sure if you are actually remote viewing or just being duped into believing you are. If you have very little natural talent, or aren't cut out for this stuff, then it's better you find that out up front instead of later. It can be a very expensive experience otherwise.

4. Don't cheat. The only person you are fooling is your-self. It will be amply clear to those you are trying to impress later.

5. Try not to have any expectations beyond the level at which you are functioning. No one operates at a superior level of performance all the time. Think of remote viewing as hitting on a baseball team. Everyone has an expectation that you will put it out of the park every time you come to bat. However, the pros understand that "control" is everything. They'd much rather have a man who can guarantee a base hit almost every time at the plate, than some-one who puts it out of the park now and then. Don't force it.

6. Don't make unsubstantiated claims. It does severe damage to the field and will quickly establish you as a fool.

How Information Might Be Processed

No one really knows where the information comes from, how it's delivered, or how we are able to process it. There are lots of theories but no real answers. The predominant theory dictates that there is some form of emission (usually thought of as coming from the target), some kind of transfer mechanism (a transmission device or method), and some form or receiver (remote viewer). No one has a clue to the truth of this. It just seems that way.

We are stuck with our observations and logic when it comes to deciding how reality operates. We can tear it apart, down to the smallest particle (which is probably not yet small enough), but we have no real understanding of how the laws of time/space really operate. There may not be an emitter, transmission, or receiver. It may be that all are one and the same thing.

Be that as it may, I do feel we process the information in some way. This has to be done in order to either verbalize or draw something about the target. This means we think about it. Without argument, this is where the problems lie, for a number of reasons.

First, many assume the information comes in totally intact and unobstructed. This would mean the emitter, transmission, and receiver, are perfect. I doubt this. Aside from that, many assume the subconscious is the first level owner of the information and that the subconscious doesn't make mistakes; I doubt this as well. And finally, many think that you can obtain information from the subconscious and use it at the cognitive level while doing no (or at least minimal) processing, which I believe to be totally fictitious.

All this sounds pretty hopeless, doesn't it? Nevertheless, somehow we still get accurate information sometimes. How? I believe it's just the opposite of what everyone else thinks. It's because we *do* process, we *do* cogitate on what's going on inside our heads. We apply high order logic *along with feelings,* about what we are actually perceiving or knowing, which oddly seems to add sometimes, and sometimes to detract perhaps from our ability.

Logic demands that we have a selection of things to choose from. It seems that the more we add in terms of selection the worse the accuracy problem becomes. But, only on the surface is that true. It's true if we force things into our perception instead of allowing them to settle there by their own accord. We force things through assumption, so the first thing we need to do is *control assumption.*

The other side of the coin is feelings. How we feel about things we are considering. Unfortunately, it is very difficult to separate ourselves from our own needs. We have a need to be right. We want certain things as a matter of personal bias or preference. We even demand that things go a certain way when we see what the potential list of outcomes might be. These things are all ego driven. These are conscious things that are born from our personalities. So, we need to learn to *control ego*. We need to learn to control our expectation for certain outcomes and go with the flow.

If you can curb ego and prevent assumptions, in other words, buy time for open-ended processing, then you go a long way towards allowing your innate talent for psychic functioning to operate. When this is married to an appropriate protocol that "allows" psychic functioning (rather than some pseudo form of psychic functioning) the combination is dynamite. But, it is a constant war. Like the pitcher on the mound, you are always at war with yourself, with control, in the search for the perfect game.

Techniques for Fooling the Conscious Mind (Ego)

Over the years, I've developed a number of techniques for fooling my ego or conscious mind, for lulling it to sleep while I attempt to produce psychic information. I have no idea if these will work for anyone else, but I list these here in the event they may.

1. Give your waking mind a menial task to keep it busy. Not something too difficult, but something that keeps it generally focused away from what you are trying to do remote viewing-wise. Pulling weeds in the garden, raking leaves, sketching a work of art, hiking in the woods, or, when trapped at a desk in an office, doodling. Anything that gives your active and awake mind something to deal with.

2. Develop an attitude that success or failure is not the measure by which you will judge your efforts. Judge your efforts on your ability to clear your mind, center

your thoughts, meet the challenge, and glean as much from the experience as you possibly can. Don't think about being right, think about doing the right thing, honoring the skill, and accepting whatever you are gifted with in response. You don't feel a need to prove you can actually taste strawberries, do you? Ignore the need to demonstrate your psychic ability.

3. Understand that being psychic is just one innate talent. It probably takes about as much effort as playing a musical instrument, or some form of athletic prowess. The point being, there is an enormous range of talent that can be found in human kind. Allow that all human beings possess at least a few talents you yourself do not have. Bury your pride and acknowledge the skills in others. When you automatically respect another human, honor them above yourself regardless of their form of innate talent, you will know you are winning the battle.

4. Give up the idea that you will ever have the perfect answer or the total answer delivered to you on a platter. Lose your need for a conclusion, and automatically trash your assumptions. Bits and pieces—these are the skills of a psychic. You should not even be trying to determine what they mean in the scheme of things. Think of yourself as a conduit for unattached information. When you can do that, it will flow.

Processing Material

I can only share what I do. I've spent twenty-one years developing a processing model in my head that seems to work for me about as well as anything might. It goes something like the following.

When something, a word, phrase, pictogram, or thought comes into my mind, I file it categorically as just that—a word, a phrase, a pictogram or thought. Initially, I give it no further consideration. I then "re-taste" the target by opening to it again. I view each re-taste as different from any other. I do not assume that I'm getting the same thing, and I do not assume that anything I get will match or go with anything else I've previously gotten. I do this very rapidly three or four times. This begins to produce a feeling regarding the target, an overall concept—what we call a gestalt. Perhaps it's a feeling of a beach, perhaps a beach with some kind of a commercial flavor to it. I then go back and begin to look at specific items I've categorized or filed. Within the context of feeling, some might support one another. I make these initial, tentative combinations, and re-file them as just that—tentative. I begin the re-tasting of the target over and over again. I begin to receive more complex data at this point.

I believe that this is so because I've been able to lay a soft underpinning for the kind of structure my mind wants to build which will tell me more about the target. In most cases when I'm doing this for research, I don't have to go much further, since all that is necessary is a very good gestalt, with good detail, to provide the kind of data that's necessary to support the on-going study. In the case of applications, however, it is a repetitive process that begins to build more and more of a structure regarding the target, eventually producing enough data in my mind for a more cohesive picture to form. This process is never forced, driven, or overlaid with my own expectations. It is allowed to slowly and methodically crunch along till something is produced of it's own accord. I myself am usually totally surprised by the end result. The more surprised I am, the better I know it's going to be.

A lot of times I'm asked if I can tell the difference between good and bad remote viewing. The answer is no.

However, if I'm totally surprised by the result, I can almost assure you that it will be good information.

Analyzing the Material

Remote viewers should never analyze their own material. Let someone else do that. This is especially pertinent to the learning process. There are a lot of reasons why, and I will share the most important ones in order of importance.

1. You are attempting to defeat your ego by training yourself not to make assumptions or jump to conclusions about remote viewing material or input. By analyzing your own material, you are simply turning around and reinforcing the need for assumptions and conclusions. How crazy is that?

2. Regardless of what anyone tells you, you haven't a clue as to what is right or what is wrong about your material. At least someone who is privy to the actual target has some idea what should fit. So, let them do the analysis. If you become privy to what the target is, you have just given up any hope of ever re-visiting it, at least in the very near future.

3. As a remote viewer, you are tasked with analyzing and taking command of your internal workings, your internalized processing methods; remote viewing accuracy on the other hand, is assisted by someone who analyzes you. This takes an independent observer, someone separate from yourself. Over time, this person can recognize habits and things you would never recognize about yourself. Over time, they come to understand those tiny quirks in you that tell them when you are operating at your peak

or operating in your valley. This assists substantially in the evaluation of material for use.

Record Keeping

Probably no aspect of learning to be a remote viewer is more important than record keeping. Psychologists will be the first to tell you that the way we remember things is generally not the way or sequence in which they happened. All human beings have selective memory. Our brains operate that way. It is meant to optimize our ability to survive, to categorize the things that are more important and more valuable to us, all within a framework that alters with a person's age. We are constantly compensating for change.

So, at a minimum, remote viewers should keep a log of all of their activities. This is hard to do. I myself violate it just about as much as the next person. But, if you rely on your memory, you will be betrayed. I recommend this log be a permanently bound book, like a diary, as you will be less inclined to pull pages out of it, or attempt to modify something within it. When I keep a log, I try to use a lab notebook that has numbered pages and is permanently bound. It's pretty much impossible to mix a sequence of events that way.

The person who runs the training should also keep a very detailed event log, with cross-referenced file numbers. If they don't, you really can't trust their memory either. Usually this habit helps to separate the real trainers from the "wannabes." They have to take the lumps and failures in their training techniques, just as the viewer does. Be very suspicious of anyone who shows you a log of events that is nearly perfect. I've been operating in a science environment for over fourteen years and I can tell you that as hard as one might try to insure that everything goes about as near perfect as possible, things always go wrong. That should be part of the record. It has a lot to do with everyone learning all they can about remote viewing, not just the viewing parts. It's through these records that progress is eventually made. Recurring errors in protocol, sequence, or possible information leakage paths will pop out at you when you've got the logs to study. All this goes to creating a system that is airtight and improved. The tighter the system is the higher the likelihood for success. Write everything down. In the end you will never be sorry that you did.

(Note: Keeping a personal journal is of value for a lot more reasons than just remote viewing training. It gives you a solid reference for reflection on other things going on in your life. Just remember personal journals contain very sensitive information and should be handled and stored accordingly. Never give your personal journal to anyone else.)

Scientific Journal Outline

There are a number of elements, which should be contained within a formal lab report on a remote viewing. Examples of these are provided below.

Consent to Participate

This is a paper that is signed by the subject or participant showing they have been fully informed about their participating in a parapsychological experiment. The following is an example of such a form:

Intuitive Intelligence Applications, Inc.

P.O. Box 100, Nellysford, Virginia 22958

CONSENT TO PARTICIPATE IN A PROPOSED
STUDY OF REMOTE VIEWING

You are invited to participate in research intended to enhance the detection of any occurrence of Remote Viewing (RV). We anticipate that a successful study will lead to more efficient experiments to understand the possible mechanisms of RV.

Before the experiment beings, you will be given an experiment schedule of dates and locations. This experiment will involve travel to a site, or sites, designated by the lab or a client. If you accept this invitation, you will be asked to participate in ten to twenty trials from approximately January through December 1991. There will be no more than three trials per day, each of which will last approximately 15-30 minutes. For each trial, at a prearranged time, laboratory personnel will select a target binary number (i.e., photograph) from a pool of photographs and place it in a designated location at the Nellysford laboratory. This target will remain in the designated location for the duration of a trial. Receivers may have access to the target through remote viewing only. At that time, you will be asked to work with an experiment monitor in a quiet place for a period of no longer than 30 minutes. During that period you will be asked to write and draw in detail your impressions of the target material.

At the conclusion of each trial the monitor will collect and secure all of you, original written, drawn, or recorded RV responses. The experiment monitor will then provide a copy of the target photograph as trial feedback.

At the conclusion of the study, you will be told the details of the analysis, the statistical outcome of your contribution, and the overall outcome of the experiment. The confidentiality of your participation in this experiment will be protected at all times. Your name will not be used. Reference to you in records of this experiment and in any published results will be coded or in consolidated form only.

Similar research in other laboratories has shown that no health risks are involved in participating in this type of experiment. This field of research, however, is deemed by some to have no scientific foundation. Some friends or colleagues, therefore, may consider your participating to indicate a belief in the occult or paranormal. While, to the knowledge of the investigators, no one has suffered career damage from participating in scientific research of the type we are proposing, you should realize that your credibility with some persons might be damaged if you should choose to reveal your participation in this experiment.

In addition, there is no reason to believe that, having participated in studies such as this you will be able to use your abilities for specific personal gain. Occasionally, participants come to believe that they possess the capacity to use so-called psychic skills for personal profit in risk-taking situations (e.g., participating in games of chance or speculative investments). Some individuals who have participated in experiments of this kind have acted on such assumptions to their apparent disadvantage. Thus, the risk exists that you may come to believe that you have a skill that you may not possess. You are advised of this risk and warned that you assume responsibility for any assumptions that you make about your personal skills or capabilities.

Emergency medical care is available if the need arises during your participation in this study at the Intuitive Intelligence Applications facilities in Nellysford, Virginia, we will call the Urgent Care Center of Nellysford and explain the nature of the emergency and take appropriate action if required.

If this explanation leaves you with any unanswered questions, please ask and obtain answers satisfactory to you before signing below. If you have questions later, please call Joseph W. McMoneagle at _____. Our protocols are institutionally reviewed, as is our plan of study to insure that you are protected to the maximum extent possible from any health risks that may be associated with your participation in this study. Additional inquiries or comments may be addressed to this office at any time.

Your participation in the research is voluntary. You will be free to cease participating at any time. If you decide to participate or you later withdraw from participation, there will be no adverse consequences to you.

After receiving the information provided above and the answers to my questions, I, _____ agree to participate as a subject in the activity described. I consent to the use of and publication of any data or information resulting from my participation, provided that I am not personally identified. I further understand that additional information regarding the experiment will be available to me on request and that I may withdraw my consent to participate in this experiment at any time. I am an adult and am not presently under medication or treatment by a physician, except

_____.

You signature indicates that you have read and understood the above information, that your questions have been answered to your satisfaction, and that you have decided to participate based on the information provided. A copy of this form will be furnished to you.

_____   _____
Signature of Subject   Signature of Witness

_____
Signature of Principal Investigator

_____
Date

Record of Experiment

This is a sheet, that becomes a permanent part of the experimental file and records the minimum data required by the lab for historical and study purposes. The following is an example of such a sheet:

EXPERIMENT INFORMATION SHEET

DATE:_____

PRINCIPAL INVESTIGATOR: _____

MONITOR: _____

SUBJECT:_____

PLACE OF EXPERIMENT: _____

TIME STARTED: _____ TIME STOPPED: _____

CONSENT FORM SIGNED: _____
(Yes)(Date)

SPECIFIC TARGETING MATERIALS PROVIDED TO VIEWER:

_____

_____

_____

_____

FEEDBACK PROVIDED: _____

_____

_____

_____

_____

OTHER COMMENTS:

_____

_____

_____

_____

MATERIALS RECORDED: _____ _____
                                    Date   Time

_____ _____

Monitor Signature   Witness Signature

Specific Targeting Material Used

This targeting material should be referred to as: "Sealed envelope: A001389"

This original sealed envelope would be verified still sealed by the witness when the remote viewing session material is recorded. It is then provided to the remote viewer for feedback.

(Care is always taken to differentiate between the actual material that is provided to the viewer for remote viewing purposes, and what was actually inside the envelope. What was actually inside the envelope will be noted as the specific "feedback" provided to the viewer in this case.)

In research circumstances where a photograph may have been sealed within the envelope, this photograph is only provided to the viewer for feedback after the judging has been accomplished. This precludes an information leakage path that could exist between the person who is evaluating the remote viewing and the remote viewing itself.

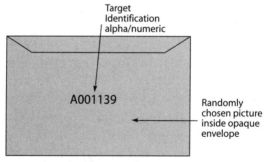

Example of the targeted envelope

Directions: Describe where this person is standing

**Example of the information
contained within the targeted envelope**

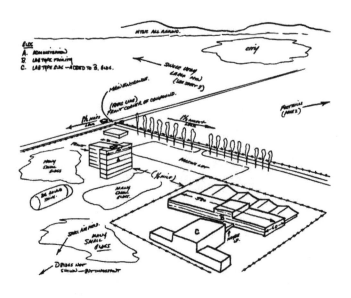

Example of Viewer data collected

[handwritten text, partially legible:]
T Shaped Administration type of building, in
a congested high tech area. (BLDG A)
Freel building is called "Building A."
Major town (Bedroom community somewhere off
to the Upper right area off a main road.
Building C is more of a manufacturing
area of some sort when I get a story line

(Unlike this example: All of the remote viewing data
that is produced is logged in and stored, to include data
that isn't pertinent or might have been inaccurate.
Nothing is ever discarded in research.)

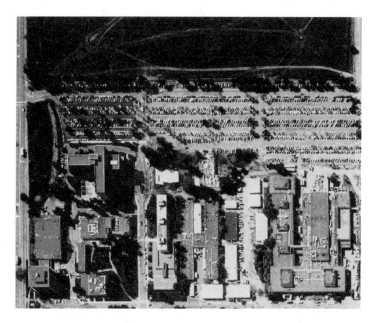

Example of feedback provided to remote viewer

Suggested Pre-Viewing Checklist

Just before you do a remote viewing, there are a number of things you should be asking yourself.

With regard to research or applications, if you have an affirmative response to any of these questions, except perhaps numbers twelve and fifteen, you might want to think about delaying or putting off the remote viewing until a later time.

With regard to training, you can view the checklist as a way to actually test which of these things might irritate you to the point of failure, or as part of the "learning-to-operate-under-most-conditions" condition.

Aside from number four, which you can't biologically avoid, I trained without the checklist. By doing so, I learned to overcome the possible irritations that can interfere with remote viewing.

1. Am I hungry?

2. Am I thirsty?

3. Am I uncomfortable?

4. Do I have to use the bathroom?

5. Is there an irritating or repetitive noise present?

6. Am I anxious about anything? (remote viewing doesn't count.)

7. Am I upset about anything?

8. Am I angry about anything?

9. Am I abnormally worried about anything?

10. Are there pets present that will interfere?

11. Are there people present that will interfere?

12. Can the phones ring?

13. Do I expect any guests in the immediate future?

14. Do I need pens, pencils, paper, or other materials?

15. Is the ambient light too bright?

16. Are there any distractions in the room?

Example of a Small Training Target Pool

The following is an example of a small target pool for training purposes. The pictures demonstrate the kinds of things that make good targets.

(Cave)A1

(Church Steeple)A2

(Church)A3

(Cliff Near Water)B1

(Domed Building)B2

(Hillside House)B3

(Indian Ruins)C1

(Mountain Top)C2

(Mount Rushmore)C3

(Pier)D1

(Rocky Shore Line)D2

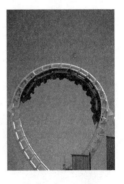

(Roller Coaster)D3

(Statue Against Wall)E1

(Strip Mine)E2

(Tall Building)E3

(Unique Building)F1

(Unique Building)F2

(Waterfall)F3

Chapter Eight

※

Applications

How long does it take to become a remote viewer? A day? A week? Longer? The real answer lies in competence. Theoretically, one could walk into a lab and within three hours, do a very respectable remote viewing. In my observation, this has happened frequently. Remember, remote viewing is just another sense, like taste or sight. Where the difficulty enters is surrounding competence, dependability, and/or stability.

In STARGATE we never considered anyone a remote viewer until s/he finished training. But, training in our program was almost always a minimum of anywhere from three to eighteen months, usually depending upon how much innate talent the person had walking through the door. Someone with a lot of natural talent could usually be quite productive within ninety days. Those with very little either took the full term of training, or failed to complete it. (Yes, we did have those too.)

In my own opinion, you can't really base it on training at all. In my own mind, I've been training now for almost twenty-two years, and I expect as long as I want to play in this game I'll always be training to some extent. So, the word "training" really doesn't work for me when it comes to calling someone a remote viewer. This is especially true since so many bogus training shops opened following the release of the original remote viewing information to the press on *Nightline* in 1995.

I would probably use the following criteria to identify someone as a real remote viewer:

1. *Performance.* Being able to demonstrate remote viewing ability over a length of time (*probably exceeding a year*), while consistently maintaining a hit rate in excess of chance. This automatically implies some form of testing, which takes into account a measurement of accuracy and statistics based on a scientific methodology. Unfortunately, while scientific labs all do that, most do not have access to scientific labs. Almost without exception, most people who are trained as viewers are into applications, or are trained by those who are focused on applications. In order not to slight those who are very good viewers and have no access to such a lab, I would modify this requirement to include any form of "testing" that mimics a scientific evaluation, where they can prove a statistical hit rate of any kind within an acceptable protocol. I would not relax this requirement to include "hits" within applications scenarios for obvious reasons—they are uncontrolled and the evaluation is subjective.

2. *Contribution to the field.* A remote viewer should provide something meaningful to the field of remote viewing, either in helping to understand it or as subjects through participation. Lip service doesn't count. Neither do bragging rights or tall tales of derring-do. Actively participating in a way that is injurious or damaging to the field should be reason for expulsion.

3. *Adherence to protocol.* Like all good clubs or associations, you can prove your mettle by showing that

you not only understand the rules and know why they exist, but that you clearly understand what a protocol is. You must live by these rules and defend them. This sometimes takes a lot more courage than many are willing to expend.

Applications

If you've been well trained, there should be an almost seamless transfer from training targets to applications types of targets. The difficulty will be that the people providing you with the target will know very little or almost nothing about them as well. Which, if you understand anything about what I've said so far, should make obtaining the information even easier.

A really good applications target is a target that someone knows at least something about, but needs additional information in order to make some kind of a decision in reference to it. Since remote viewing is never meant to stand alone in providing such information, it is best used where it can assist in pointing to a more direct way of knowing, or a more direct way of obtaining that which you would like to know.

As an example, let's say I have a Boeing 727, which I know has just been put through a severe shaking. Perhaps it was in route from Panama to Miami, when the pilot had to make a sudden course correction to avoid hitting a smaller plane. Most aircraft can take quite a beating, but it's always good to really check them over thoroughly after such an occurrence; besides, regulation dictates it. How would I benefit through the use of remote viewing? I know I have to pretty much X-ray their entire inaccessible portion of the plane for possible stress fractures. So, how would remote viewing reduce that cost?

To begin, there are certain givens. (Having expertise in aircraft, I can winnow down the areas that are most critical, and probably deserve a first peek, to maybe seven.) Since I know a lot about the aircraft, I already also know where previous repairs have been made, or there are previous problems noted in the logbook. So, there is considerable information available. Now, I'd like to bring in a viewer to reduce my costs further.

I take an instant photo of the specific plane with tail markings, write, "identify possible damage" on the back side, and put it into an envelope. I then ask a remote viewer to tell me what I want to know about the target in the envelope.

S/he gives me a very crude drawing of what I know appears to be the intersection of a main wing strut with the fuselage. That would be the first place I would X-ray.

Critics might say, "Well, you have to X-ray the whole aircraft anyway, so where's the savings in using a viewer?" This is true, if you have to X-ray the entire aircraft. But, what if that's where the most severe damage is, and you locate it first? Maybe repairing the damage exceeds the value of the plane, so you decide to write it off. You just saved the cost of all those other X-rays, man-hours in the maintenance bay, etc.

In truth, there's probably a 60/40 chance at minimum, the remote viewing is going to help. For a few hundred dollars, doesn't it seem worth it?

Or, maybe you get word that some terrorist organization crossed a border somewhere in the continental United States, with a weapon of mass destruction. Your problem is that this could have taken place over a twelve-hour period. Even if you knew where they crossed the border, you still have a minimum of seven to ten states to search, an overwhelming task. What you are really up against, aside from finding them, is time. The more time it takes you to find them, the higher the likelihood they will succeed in their mission.

As with the Boeing 727, a viewer can sometimes reduce your search area by 80% immediately. A 60/40 chance, on the up side that the viewer will be correct you say? Well, I'd want that advantage. No one knows where to start in the first place, so you might as well be where you have a 60/40 chance of finding the terrorists first. Any increase in odds could mean the difference between success and failure with regard to time. In the event the viewer is wrong, you would have had to search the entire area anyway.

Neither of these scenarios is meant to preclude any other form of participation or information collection and analysis. Remote viewing should be used to enhance, not detract, from whatever is required or necessary. Properly used, it can be advantageous. But, it takes an open mind and an inventive mind to structure the approach.

Some targets are better than others for use in an applications type of effort, and they will almost always be the types of targets where at least something is known and you are looking to fill in an unknown or gap. There are a number of reasons for this.

If you know something about the target in the first place, then when the remote viewer provides information it is easier to see how it might fit within the target overall. It also provides enough information to assist in evaluating the rest of the material the viewer is providing.

Going back to the example of the Boeing 727, if the viewer is totally blind to the target and the information they provide is clearly pertinent to an aircraft, then you can assume the target has been acquired. It's even better if you have lots of background information about a Boeing 727, and many of the details you already know about the plane begin to match the viewer's information. This is not only a clear indication that the viewer has acquired the target appropriately, but that they have also made contact with a 727. So, when you need to evaluate the portion of the material that you don't know anything about, you are more inclined to understand its quality or probable accuracy.

If the information the viewer provides doesn't match anything like a Boeing 727, then you can safely say no contact was made with the target, and then re-target, or go to another viewer.

In this context, it is easy to see why you might have difficulty trusting the information provided by viewers when they are front-loaded with foreknowledge of the target. Simply telling the viewer that it is an aircraft from the outset, "to save time" is the usual excuse, destroys any possibility of using known information to confirm the unknown information when the effort is evaluated or analyzed.

There are application types of targets where very little is known. Since so very little is known, one should take even more care to guarantee that prior knowledge about such targets does not reach the viewer. Otherwise there will be almost no means left by which to evaluate the material.

Of course there is another way to try to confirm whether or not a viewer is on the target. One could conceivably bracket a tough or almost unknown target with two targets that you know everything about. Essentially ask the remote viewer to do all three, then assume that the accuracy of the real target is at least as good as the two you can evaluate. But you've automatically increased the workload three-fold, which further reduces the expectation for success. Not something you want to do except as a last resort.

So, for applications, contrary to general opinion, blind targeting is almost a necessity. The remote viewer should know little or nothing about the actual target.

Double-Blind

There is also something known as "double blind." That's where no one who actually works the problem knows anything about the target. The target is set up as a sealed and opaque envelope and delivered to the persons who will actually interact with the person interacting with the remote viewer.

In applications scenarios, double blind is almost never used, mostly because it requires a third layer of people within the remote viewing collection system. This extra layer of people represents additional requirements for expertise that is already hard to come by, as well as a much greater degree of expense.

Nevertheless, there are times when such a demand is made. Usually this has nothing to do with the specific target that is being dealt with, but it has everything to do with the "belief" of those who will eventually deal with the results.

There is a lot of self-imposed fear surrounding an application that requires a double blind, especially from the viewers. They feel that establishing such a requirement is a less than subtle comment about how far someone is willing to trust them, or that it in some way implies they are dishonest. I have done hundreds if not a thousand double blind targets in research as well as applications and have never been offended. Statistically they fall within about the same parameters as blind targets and are generally no more difficult.

Having said that, I can also say that when it comes to applications, double blind targeting is probably unnecessary except in extreme cases where proof of principle is required to convince a new player or user in the remote viewing field. Double blind targeting will always be essential within the structure of research. In other words, if you want to be a remote viewer and expect to play on the research side of the house, then you will have to get used to it, especially if you are going to have any sensitivity to such things.

Front-Loading

Front-loading is an interesting term that was born out of remote viewing as it was being pursued with regard to applications only. After some years of effort, it was believed by many that in order to cut to the quick of a problem and not waste time with parts of the target that weren't material, you could simply "front load" the remote viewer. That is, provide remote viewers with a minimal amount of information pertinent to the target, which would get them to the important area of interest faster.

There is nothing wrong with this in theory, but there is a lot wrong in practice. It takes someone with profound expertise in the transfer of information—one human to another—to understand when they might be doing it inappropriately. We'd all like to think we know when that happens, but the fact of the matter is that we don't. What usually happens is that the viewer is told too much about the target. This injects an enormous amount of overlay and inventive creation into the process. It then becomes very difficult to differentiate between what is truly psychic information, and information that is solely based on logic. Some feel that it doesn't matter. And in the end it may not, if you achieve what you are hoping to achieve. But, in such a case you cannot state that it was remote viewing (psychic material) that saved the day. This encourages improper use of the remote viewers, teaches them dependence on front loading, and ultimately results in remote viewing being oversold.

Using the example of our 727 jet aircraft, you can probably get away with telling the viewer it's an aircraft. You might even get away with saying you are primarily interested in the center section of the aircraft. But, telling the viewer that you are interested in any damage to an aircraft would be too much front loading. If there is no damage, the viewer will probably invent some. There's a risk of that in any event, just front-loading them with knowledge that it's an aircraft.

The time that front loading might be used in a very positive way would be in answering a question about a target without them knowing what the target is. Again, using the 727 as an example: "There is a picture of an object in this envelope. We want to know anything you can tell us about the object's structure that might be important to us."

What's important is whether or not there is significant structural damage. In this case the result is being driven by both the intentions and the expectations for a specific kind of outcome, neither of which has to be spoken aloud to anyone directly connected to the actual remote viewing.

The most important things to remember about front-loading are the following:

1. It should be used sparingly, if at all.

2. If you do not have a minimum of at least three years' experience tasking remote viewers, you probably shouldn't be front-loading them.

3. There is a very grave risk that you will be doing more damage than good by front-loading.

4. If there is doubt in the result, discard it and re-approach the target using a different viewer.

Multiple Remote Viewings

When targeting the same viewer against a target s/he has already worked, many feel very strongly that the viewer should know what s/he said or didn't say that was right about the target in the first viewing. Their reasoning appears to be sound. The viewer got the information in the first place. Positive feedback encourages the viewer to be more productive and helps him or her focus on what's more important. The problem is they are also being told what they got wrong, which thoroughly frames the targeted with respect to what is desired and is the worst kind of front loading.

If you are going to re-visit a target with the same viewers, you can use the material they gave you to direct them, but you can't tell them why. In other words, you can't tell them what they might have gotten right or wrong about the target. The reason is simple. By doing so, you are encouraging them to rely on logic, based on what they know is now right or wrong about the target, than to rely on their innate psychic ability.

Using the Boeing 727 again as an example, let's say a viewer has provided a fairly accurate drawing of a primary wing strut and how it connects to the main fuselage. Let's say there is an indication in the drawing that there might be a section that's damaged, but without more information it's hard to tell. If you have already told the viewer generally that s/he drew fairly accurate drawings of the aircraft, when s/he revisits them in a later remote viewing session s/he will be more inclined to not add to or change what they have already drawn. Since s/he doesn't know specifically what's right or wrong about the drawings or transcript, s/he won't want to alter them. If you say specifically what's right or wrong about the drawings, s/he will want to add what logically "seems" to be missing. This distracts from actual psychic information, or at the very least turns it into a forced-choice test. As everyone knows, forced choice almost never works well. If you have said nothing, s/he is more inclined to go back to satisfying the unspoken intention and expectation, or reason for the remote viewing in the first place.

By not saying anything about accuracy, you can then point to something in the original session's drawings or transcripts, and ask him or her to "expand on that area."

This sort of implies there might be something there that's important, but doesn't say what it is. It encourages the viewer to search for something connected to what's there, but which s/he figure s/he has not yet seen. A subtle difference, but in this business, subtlety is everything. It separates the reality from fantasy and illusion.

If care is taken, the same remote viewer can re-visit the same target many times. You have only to say, "refocus on this area you told us about," and point to something on the drawings, or in the verbal transcript of the previous viewing. It actually makes the later feedback a lot more meaningful.

Working Alone as a Viewer

There really is no such thing as working totally alone. That implies that the viewer has absolutely no one else helping them. While I usually do all of the actual remote viewing alone, there are two forms of support structure I use dependent upon whether or not it is a research target or an application one.

A research target is almost always somewhere else. That means the sealed envelope, photograph, person's name, event title, whatever, is always somewhere else where I can't actually see it. I'm usually told where it is—on the computer screen, in an envelope on someone's desk—or simply that's it's been prepared specifically for me and they now have an expectation that I will produce a result that will answer their questions. So, in a sense I'm not working alone, as someone else is actually responsible for the target, preparing it in some way, or directing me to it.

In applications, which always take place in my proximity, my wife always decides how the target will be presented. For over ten years she has been preparing my targets for me. These are almost always wrapped very carefully within an inner sheet and then sealed well inside an envelope, usually the kind a banker would use which you can't read through. I never break the seal, nor do I ever open the envelope, even when I'm through. I return it in the same condition along with the remote viewing information. She may reframe the basic viewing information in direct response to the original requestor's questions.

This is absolutely essential for a number of reasons. Primarily, if the customer wants me to look at the issue again, then I can without any problem. Also, they may decide that I did not really answer their question appropriately and may want me to take another look at it. I never assume that because I'm looking at the same target again, I didn't do something right. I assume nothing about my work at all. I always let someone else tell me how good or how bad it was when it has been completed. In all cases, I do not discuss what I do for private customers, whether or not they are people or businesses. Occasionally I've asked for permission, but in all cases where permission was not granted, I do not ask again, nor do I violate the requirement for total confidentiality. This has frustrated some magazine, television, or newspaper writers who would like to use examples of my work, but that's too bad.

Chapter Nine

—— ✳ ——

Time

There are a lot of very strange beliefs floating about regarding time and its influence on remote viewing. I've heard people say you can't go back in time much farther than the beginning of the first observer. They obviously believe it is telepathy; someone had to be present to observe something, if any information is going to be transferred. Others have said you can't go forward any farther than 2012, 2025, 2500, etc. They believe this for a multitude of reasons: the way certain calendars will end, Extra-Terrestrials (ETs) being a major preventative cause, and even God denying access to the material. The truth of the matter is, no one really knows.

Historically I guess, one would have to say that it depends on how far you can stretch your belief, or proof in principle; in other words, what one has observed to be true. So, one thing is for sure, if it doesn't happen in your personal lifetime, then it probably isn't going to be taken very seriously. What the heck, we won't be here, right? But shouldn't we find a reason to believe? Shouldn't we be concerned about a future we might not even experience? I think we should if for no other reason than what we might be leaving to our children, perhaps a planet poisoned by gases, severe over-population, or corrupted weather patterns.

The facts in the matter are scarce and sometimes complicated. But, I will share what my experience has shown me to be true.

Present Time

As I explained in my book, *The Ultimate Time Machine*, there probably isn't any thing like the present. We fool ourselves into believing there is, in order to adjust and recognize our place in reality. It helps us to locate where we are in time/space. Be that as it may, present time does imply something happening, or an object/thing existing relatively close to where we are in time. It involves where people might be as we are thinking about them, what events might be occurring, or what object/thing might be perceived at a location remote from us as at the same moment. It is very easy to target these things, not because they are easier to remote view than most other targets, but because our "belief systems" allow us to buy it as real.

Think about it for a moment. Some people are willing to buy the ability to describe an event, person, object, place, or thing totally chosen at random and to which we have absolutely no other form of access in real time, but, these same people will reject the notion of past or future targeting. Why? Doesn't make any sense, does it?

Actually, the problem lies in one's ability to rationalize. You can rationalize the existence of the target in your own time frame, but you can't in a time frame for which you have no knowledge. Not surprising really. In other words, you are willing to suspend your disbelief only so far. You are willing to agree to psychic functioning, but not to time warping.

What if I told you that, in my experience, most remote viewers who target something in the present usually provide some information that is pertinent to the target in the past and future? Well, that's exactly what happens in most cases. The first target I ever did worked that way, and I'm sure it won't be the last. I saw a red bicycle in a bicycle rack outside the front door of the target building. The outbounder didn't see one, because no bicycle was there when it was being targeted. But, when the remote viewing was completed and we all went back to the target for my feedback, someone rode in on a red bicycle and parked it in the rack, sort of fulfilling the prophecy.

There are numerous examples of information being provided by viewers on present-time targets, where the information was slightly off in one direction or another. It's always been fascinating to me that no one ever talks about the phenomenon, nor do they take the past/future information into account when trying to evaluate how or why remote viewing works.

One thing can be said about real time targets: they may predominantly lie within real time, but they will usually contain near past and near future information as well. This means that fixing a target in time is critically important to the remote viewing process. The more accurately you can do that the better.

By necessity, when targeting something in present time, or for that matter, in the past or future, you should provide one of the following statements:

1. Describe the target, as it exists now.

2. We want to know about the target, as it exists today, July 14, 1999, at 10:15 A.M..

3. Our interest lies in present time only.

I once did a whole series of targets at SRI-International for which no specific time of interest was mentioned. Every single one failed. It was years later that buildings I had described in those remote-viewing sessions were actually built at those specific target sites.

Past Targets

The primary belief about past targets deals with telepathy. Many who buy remote viewing as possible do not believe you can remote view past a point where there was human consciousness present. You need at least one mind to transmit the information to another mind. This is a great hypothesis, provided you buy into the belief that most or at least some of the information transferred is through telepathy. The thing that complicates this is that both elements are probably true. I'm convinced that at least a part of the information being passed comes through telepathy. But, I would disagree that this makes telepathy necessary to remote viewing.

I think remote viewing uses whatever lines of communication or information resources that are available. When there is no line of information available through telepathy, it looks elsewhere.

Unfortunately, there is very little evidence that I can offer. I could ask Christians, if this is so, then where did the information come from. . . reference creation prior to the existence of Adam or Eve in the Bible? Oh, that's right, it was inspired by the word of God. Okay, isn't God an intelligent entity? I'm not proposing that God gives information to remote viewers, I'm just questioning how we think about consciousness, knowledge, how or where it might all come from. Seems to me that in our bungling nature, we would be somewhat arrogant in claiming to know all sources of knowledge or how information might be shared or generated throughout the cosmos. But, these are just my thoughts.

To state it more emphatically, I have seen absolutely no evidence that limits the ability to remote view into the past, other than our ability to believe that it can be done. Usually information about the past will be generated for which there is very little knowledge available in present form.

Sometimes it will take years to prove that the information was correct. Eventually, in many cases, it is proven to be correct. In numerous cases I have waited fourteen to seventeen years for confirmation on a remote viewing of the past. It's no less satisfying to see that one was right sixteen years later than in real time. Which of course points out a small twist to past targets: maybe the act of telepathy is totally within one's self. Eventually, when we find out we are right, maybe that's when we send the information to ourselves in the past. So, the confirming data from the future provides the accurate information about the past, or at least what we are willing to believe is accurate.

It may be that remote viewing information about the past is stuck within the reality of "our own time." In other words, it is only considered real because that is the consensus of the time in which it was produced. A remote viewer puts the beginning of formal metallurgy at around 120 thousand years. Current belief is 80 thousand. Proof is discovered ten years later that it's 120 thousand. The viewer is considered right. Seventy-five years later, the viewer is dead, and archeologists successfully prove that it's actually 220 thousand. So, the information is only valid during the knowledge period of the viewer. I don't know if this is how it works, but wouldn't be interesting if it is?

So, when working past targets, you should identify them as well as you would a present target (see 1, 2, and 3 above). But I need to add a cautionary note here. If you generally target someone in the past and want to depend on the date they give you, you want to be very careful about what you do with it. In my experience, and the experience of nearly all the people who know anything at all about remote viewing, you cannot depend on dates or times a remote viewer might provide. Only in the rarest of cases can a remote viewing provide a date or time that is more than general, in the extreme. It is one of the least dependable products.

Future Targets

You can't remote view past the end of the Mayan Calendar.

Someone actually said this to me at a lecture I gave in Lynchburg, Virginia. To which I replied; "You could be right, but I seriously doubt it." In reality, no one knows how far out into the future one can remote view and still produce accurate information.

Essentially remote viewing the future is the same as making a prediction. You are either predicting that something will happen, or that something will be known, at some future date and time, which accurately matches what was said in the remote viewing. Many have major hang-ups with this reality.

Most of the problems involve probabilities, a belief in multiple universes, multiple strings of reality, or things being predetermined. Of course things being preset or predetermined would imply that we all have no free will and therefore one of the major tenants of our religious belief as well as belief about our own god-like nature would be destroyed.

Well, you needn't worry because remote viewing the future doesn't imply any of that at all. If it does, then you are taking remote viewing and predictions far too seriously. Imagine yourself as a single point on a sheet of white paper, dead center. That's where you are now. Each molecule in the sheet of paper is a connective act that forms a string we call life. This would be a line that connects the dot where it lies in the center to somewhere else at some future date on the sheet. How could one possibly predict where on the sheet that second dot might lie?

I happen to believe you can, to some degree of accuracy. I base that belief on having done it, but admittedly, only locally, or in what might be assumed to be near-real time. Was I making a statement that was preordained to become true? In other words, was I establishing a predetermined outcome for someone or something? No. I was simply correct in my guess about where that point would fall on the sheet of paper. One could draw a circle, using a compass, by placing the point of the compass on the originating point and passing the line of the pencil through the second point on the paper. All the molecules contained within that circle represent all the probable or possible routes that could have been taken out to the line drawn. All the molecules falling immediately on the line represent all the possible outcomes. The only thing that can be said about a prediction that comes true in the future is that the remote viewer "did something really amazing." In such a case, all the possible outcomes represent the multitude of possibilities that occur by chance. Compared against a viewer's single guess, it is truly amazing that such a prediction could be made accurately. I guess it's clear to see why it's easier to believe a predetermined future exists, than it is to believe it's the other way around.

Ingo Swann, a well-known psychic and remote viewer with the laboratory at SRI-International, and one of the original participants in the CIA evaluations of remote viewing back in the early 1970s, made astounding predictions concerning the outlying planets in our solar system. He made these predictions up to two years prior to these planets being first visited by deep space explorer/information collection satellites. There was no significant decline in his accuracy for these targets over any other targets he worked while at SRI-International.

Literally dozens of targets worked by viewers within the STARGATE Program made successful predictions relating to events involving people, places, or things, generally out to between 90 and 365 days. More than a few predictions I've made within my files are valid out to about 15-17 years. And those who have read my book *The Ultimate Time Machine* know that I'm probably going for a world record and the reason why.

If you believe in the predictions of Edgar Cayce, then you have to believe that there is a probable ceiling of about fifty or so years to accurate predictions. If you buy some of what Nostrodamus is saying, then you are increasing your ceiling of belief out to about four hundred plus years. All of this is nice, but rationally, most are only going to buy what's relative to their own lifetime, and relevant to what's going on in the framework of their belief.

So, when targeting the future, while there is probably no limit as to how far out you can go, you might want to stick with something people are going to care about that's relevant to their own time frame. Going much farther than that will usually be viewed as fantasy or science fiction.

Again, as with recommendations in items 1, 2, and 3, above, you should be as specific as possible when targeting dates and times in the future. Expect bleed-through from the immediate past as well as the immediate future within those specific time frames as well. The primary difficulties you will encounter in targeting the future will be the ability to grasp the information. You only have to go just a few years into the future to lose sight of the conceptualizations that drive what's actually going on. As an example, as a remote viewer, how would you explain a high-energy pump laser three years before it was discovered?

Chapter Ten

— ✻ —

Reporting and Formal Record Keeping

The big question here is "what's necessary?"

The rule about record keeping for research or formal studies is: keep everything. Every note, page—printed or written, every logbook, every audio or videotape, even the materials that you've totally screwed up, you keep, all appropriately labeled and filed away. In fact, you should label everything in any single category sequentially, like; audio Tape 1, 2, and 3; Logbook A, B, or C; Experimenter's Personal Diary, Edition One, Edition Two, etc. The interior pages of the logbook should be numbered and glued in, so you can easily see if pages have been removed or added later. There should be dated file records for when all the materials were made, who was present, what it pertained to, why, and if possible the expected results as well as the actual results. If you can, you should have these items initialed.

Sounds like a lot of work, and it is. But, when it comes to making claims, it is the only thing that will suffice scientifically, or in a court of law. If you have to argue discovery, you'll be glad you kept it all. If you have to defend your work against a public challenge, you'll be glad you did. If you have to defend your good name (and working in the paranormal that will always be a reality), you'll be glad that you did. But, most importantly, when you want to go back months or even years later and study the data, to see where you might have made a mistake in your thinking, or to gain insight for a possible modification to your method, it will be right there staring you in the eye. If you trust your memory, I tell you it will fail.

Record Keeping for a Typical Experiment

The experimental notebook should be firmly bound and you should not be able to remove pages from it, or add to them. It should have all the pages numbered somewhere in sequential order. These can be in Roman numerals, Arabic, written out, alphabetic; it doesn't matter as long as they have some noted sequence or unbroken chain to them. The notebook should be clearly labeled as belonging to you, or whoever is tasked with keeping the record. Notebooks are always kept in ink, not pencil. In most scientific areas, notebooks are required to be time/dated, and initialed by a second party at the end of the workday. That's all that's required.

I have my own preferences for notebooks when I'm tasked with doing something formal. I always keep my notes in black ink, as it makes better copies. I keep my notebooks labeled sequentially, Book One, Book Two, etc., although I seldom use more than a single book for any specific experiment in which I'm required to keep one. At the beginning of each day, I write down the specific date and note the location(s), as they may change. Along the left side of the page I usually enter the time for each entry or paragraph, drawing, etc. My notebooks are lined like graph paper sometimes, and sometimes like writing paper. As graph paper, they are usually quarter inch squares of light blue lines. This helps me graphically when I have to draw something to scale, or in relationship to other objects, it helps me create columns for data, or section off one element of data from another.

For a specific experiment, I list where it's taking place, the pertinent start/stop dates, and times. I list who is present and what their specific jobs are relating to the experiment, what is going to take place in the experiment (both expected as well as observed). I might make notes about how it unfolds, or details about what happens (my observations), and why the experiment is being performed. If I'm the viewer, I will usually do the remote viewing separately from the notebook, only because it is registered and filed separately.

Any videos, audiotapes, or other materials pertinent to a formal experiment should be numbered in some way that identifies them specifically to that experiment. These should be formally logged and a separate record of their existence maintained. These should be appropriately controlled and stored according to their individual requirements. These should be referenced with their control or file identifications in the notebook.

A major word of caution is required. It's okay to keep your records on a computer, but these should be *in addition to* the hard file in the notebook. If these are relied upon in lieu of the hard notebook record, then there are a number of additional requirements that need to be met.

Computer records should always be backed up and the backup copies should be maintained in a separate facility from where the computers are located. This probably should be a safety deposit box at a bank, or within a fire-rated safe somewhere off premises. These backups should be done on a day-to-day basis. Remember, this is a permanent record, so *do not rotate* the tapes, as you might do with operational software backup tapes.

Computer files should probably be copied and copies maintained by both the originator as well as a witness. The witness should not allow access to their copies of the tapes, except when they may be required in a court of law, or to validate or confirm material and statements in support of the research. As good as the equipment is today, there is always a risk that materials kept on computer media may suffer from the same hazards as notebooks. They can be lost, destroyed, or stolen. So, adequate security should be provided for.

Since we are concerned with even the handwritten notes in formal experiments, and nothing is deliberately destroyed, there are no requirements with regard to protecting trash or discarded materials.

Record Keeping for Applications

Ideally, it probably should be the same as for formal experiments, but that's usually asking too much from someone who might be operating with a single assistant, or with minimal resources. Most of the really good remote viewers I know are buried up to their eyeballs in requests for support (mostly from non-paying clients, I would add), and they just don't have time to do all the work this would entail. (It's one of the major factors in science that drives overhead through the roof. In a lab, record-keeping alone is sometimes a two-person job, something that no one outside the lab ever considers when they see the expense sheet.)

When doing an applications type of target, you don't have to keep any information other than the basics. The following is what I would consider the minimum for an applications type of target:

1. Requestor's information: that is name, address, phone numbers, contact information, specific tasking or requirement for information, any guidance sheets, materials, or facsimiles they sent pertinent to the task at hand.

2. Actual targeting information that was used to point the viewer in the right direction. How it was given to the viewer, specifically what was said or presented, any questions or inquiries that might have been shared with the viewer while s/he was working on the target.

3. What the viewer produced. This would be the only place where I would say you should keep everything. Normally, I put what I produce in a manila envelope and write the actual targeting number on the outside. The targeting number is the randomly chosen alpha/numeric identification number my wife usually writes on the outside of the targeting envelope. This then becomes the common referral number for anything pertinent to that customer or their specific remote viewing request.

4. At the end of the project, I usually do a summary sheet, which lists anything else that is not to be found in the other material that I might consider important. This might also contain small facts or comments relative to observations I might have made while doing the project; like difficulties I might have had with the target, unique features about the viewing that bring understanding or conclusions about remote viewing I might not have had prior, even random thoughts that have no apparent value, simply because I don't trust my memory, or they seemed important at the time.

5. Everyone who participated in the applications effort should be noted. Sometimes this proves of value when you need to later check a point, or try to recreate the circumstances within which something was determined.

I always provide my customer with interim and final reports on their targets. Interim reports usually aren't required unless you are re-visiting the same target, or in some way tracking an event or situation that covers a period of time, over which the customer wants to know the progress. Remember, any communications between the customer and the remote viewer is forbidden between the time the targeting materials have been passed to the viewer and the final report is mailed. So, coordinating changes in targeting based on interim reports needs to be made between the customer and someone else, not the viewer.

All my interim, as well as final reports, will include whatever drawings I have made and a detailed narrative of what I've explored. Sometimes I will deliberately cull parts or sections of the drawings if it's my perception that they would be confusing or misleading to the customer, based on the narrative. But, this is very rare. In most cases, I will use a considerable number of footnotes to try to explain why or how something might have been entering my consciousness. (For instance, sometimes it is difficult to know a group of passengers was on a bus, a train, or a plane.) I find that cautionary notes about not jumping to conclusions, or being careful in interpreting data, go a long way toward helping the customer to understand the value of remote viewing data and how or where it should be incorporated with other forms of data.

I try to keep the records of what I do for the same time limit as required for taxes—a period of six to seven years. After that, I glean whatever I might feel is important from them from a scientific or historical standpoint and then destroy them.

Security

In applications types of targeting, some things should be done to guarantee and protect one's customer—both their reputation and the content of their interests. Minimal rules which I would suggest:

1. Use the alpha/numeric target identification-number to cross-correlate all materials, but split the materials up into different files. Maintain the different files in different file cabinets, safes, or locations.

2. Shred or otherwise make unreadable, all materials, storage media, or other sources of information identifiably connected to a specific customer, which you are going to throw away, or otherwise discard. It is surprising how many companies and corporations leave themselves totally open to victimization, simply by not shredding papers they are discarding.

3. Very proprietary, close-hold, or sensitive corporate materials either passed to you by a customer, or produced on behalf of a customer should be encrypted if stored in computer media; or, as a minimum, be stored within an approved safe or security container. If it's fireproof, that's even better.

4. On completion of a project, all materials that are no longer necessary to your own operation should either be returned to the customer through secure means, or should (with their permission) be destroyed.

5. While you are doing something for a customer, the same degree of security should be provided to their materials as you would give to something you wouldn't want shared outside your own office. Lock the work away at night, don't take the work home with you, do not leave it lying about in a brief case, or at a friend's house.

6. When transmitting information, always take care that you use whatever mode of transmission is necessary

to protect the degree of sensitivity required. A rule of thumb that I've always used: if loss of the information could be life-threatening, or be devastating to a company or individual, hand deliver it. If it could really do severe damage, then use registered mail. If it would prove embarrassing to an individual or corporation, then use certified, receipt required; and in all other cases, regular First Class Mail. Always address it specifically to an individual, preferably the one who is coordinating the targeting.

7. Never discuss the target over a cell phone. Discuss it as little as possible over a regular phone. Use a fax if you have to. Break it up into sections over e-mail. Using the same criteria as above, if disclosure could be sensitive or devastating to your company, then never use e-mail. Never use a phone or the fax. Only communicate in person, or through certified or registered mail.

There are also physical security concerns, but these are too diverse to be addressed specifically within this book. Usually, you can let common sense prevail. When in doubt, it's best to err on the safe side.

Chapter Eleven

———— ✻ ————

Unique and Strange Things Known About Remote Viewing

Some very strange things are known about remote viewing. Some we know quite a bit about, others are being tested. But, all are quite unique. I've chosen to list a couple of them here not just because they are interesting in their own right, but because if they are true and are used correctly, they can have a dramatic effect on the accuracy of remote viewing.

Local Sidereal Time (LST)

The Operations Officer for the Laboratories for the Cognitive Sciences Laboratory (CSL), S. James P. Spottiswoode, recognized an apparent association between the effect sizes in free response anomalous cognition experiments and local Sidereal time.

Note: The term "free response anomalous cognition" is the term used in CSL to denote psychic functioning under controls (to include remote viewing).

Local Sidereal time is better known as Solar time. Solar time runs on a twenty-four-hour clock, but is actually a few minutes slower than our normal clock time each day, so 12:00 noon EST in my front yard will drop back a few minutes with every twenty-four-hour period, arriving slightly earlier each day. Solar time is also specific to where you might be standing on the planet. The data that James studied is only pertinent to the Northern hemisphere, as that is where it was collected; so what is said about local Sidereal time at the moment can only be said about that longitude-band around the world. Much of the data that was studied comes from what are considered successful remote viewing experiments. James compared an existing database of 1,468 free response trials to the specific local Sidereal time for the locations and date/times in which they were done. What he discovered was astounding. For trials that took place within one hour of 13.5 hours. Local Sidereal Time (LST), there appears to be an effect size difference of approximately 340%. This means an increase in accuracy of nearly 3.5 times the normal distribution. (For those who would like to know, this is p:0.001.)

In an attempt to validate this data, James then put together an independent database of 1,015 similar trials, which were compared to the twenty-four LST clock, and these showed (within one hour of 13.5 hour LST) an effect size increase of 450% (p:0.05), confirming the effect.

He also studied possible artifacts due to the non-uniform distribution of trials in clock time and variations of effect size with experiment, rejecting these as explanations for the finding. His conclusion is that, "assuming that some unknown systematic bias is not present in the data, it appears that Anomalous Cognition performance is strongly dependent upon the LST at which the trial occurs." This means there is strong evidence suggesting a cause and effect relationship between a remote viewer's (or psychic's) performance and where they are standing and at what time on the planet's surface.

The following graph depicts what Local Sidereal Time

actually looks like for my location (at 37 degrees North Latitude) for the period January of 1997 through the end of the year.

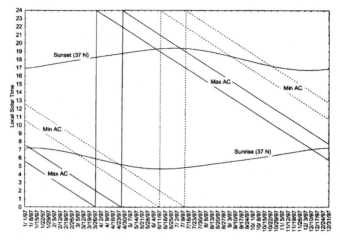

With Permission of CSL

The left column of numbers represents the twenty-four-hour clock we operate by. The bottom numbers are obviously the dates of months, scattered throughout the year. The wavy horizontal lines represent Sunrise and Sunset. They are wavy because of seasonal differences. Max AC lines bracket the one-hour window of time just before and just after 13.5 hours Local Sidereal Time for each period during the year. This would be the most opportune moment to be remote viewing. The Min AC, are times that coincide with valleys in the LST Chart, which we know corresponds with very little or no anomalous cognition taking place.

So, as an example, if I had to do a remote viewing on May the 12th of 1997, it would have been better to have been doing it between 9:00 P.M. and 11:00 P.M. Attempting to remote view between 2:00 P.M. and 4:00 P.M. that day probably would not have yielded very good results.

Another way of viewing what's going on here is to see how this relates to where you might be standing and where the earth horizon is in relationship to the core of the Milky Way.

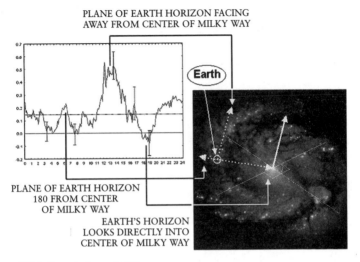

PLANE OF EARTH HORIZON FACING
AWAY FROM CENTER OF MILKY WAY

PLANE OF EARTH HORIZON
180 FROM CENTER
OF MILKY WAY

EARTH'S HORIZON
LOOKS DIRECTLY INTO
CENTER OF MILKY WAY

With Permission of CSL

When your exposure to the plane of the Milky Way is away from its core, there is an almost five-fold increase in remote viewing accuracy.

Does this mean that the stars have a direct effect on remote viewing or other forms of psychic functioning? No one knows. It could be directly related to almost anything. Just because we notice the effect to be a correlation of our physical positioning on the planet's surface does not mean our relationship to the stars is critical. A myriad of things relate to where we are standing that probably should be considered. So, the jury is still out. But it can be said that if you are interested in doing good remote viewing, you should be paying attention to Local Sidereal Time.

A full copy of James Spottiswoode's paper can be found in Appendix B.

Effects of Noise

In an attempt to establish whether or not a correlation existed between anomalous cognition (remote viewing or other forms of free response psychic performance) and geomagnetic fluctuations (GMF) James met with mixed success. He was able to confirm such a correlation when he compared a very large database of 2,879 free response trials to the ap geomagnetic index where the free response or (anomalous cognition) effect size was -0.029 ($p:0.06$). He states that a large increase in the magnitude of the correlation was found at approximately 13 hours Local Sidereal Time (LST).

What is really nice about this specific study is that in the past there have been varying correlations to GMF found in different studies. As an example, one very large remote viewing study showed near zero overall correlation, but we now know that few of the trails within that study occurred during the critical LST time period.

In another case a comparable study had a large correlation of -0.22 and by circumstance, all the trials were conducted near 13 hours LST. In looking at the graph below, please note the significant reduction in GMF during the period of time that an expected increase in remote viewing accuracy can be expected to take place.

See how the GMF compares to the previous LST model at about 13.5 hours:

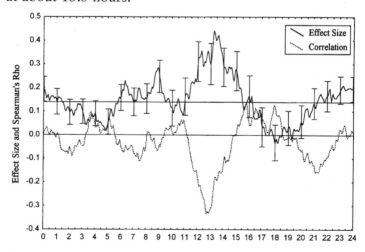

In reference to the graph above, the dotted lines represent the GMF compared to the Local Sidereal Time graph (solid line). It is apparent that when geomagnetic fluctuations are lowest, they are lowest at the same time the LST shows good remote viewing is assumed to be taking place.

A full copy of this GMF Study by James Spottiswoode is included within Appendix C.

Personal Habits

A number of personal habits impact the viewer. While none of these will actually prevent success in remote viewing, they will sometimes have a profound effect on the results, so should be mentioned.

1. **Diet.** In the past, remote viewers have reported that some things in diet have an effect on their remote viewing. There's no proof that this is so, but since some believe it does, this makes it important to a certain extent. Just about anything that increases or decreases stimulation of the nervous system could be considered contraindicated. So, consuming caffeine or alcohol is probably not a good idea. Another issue has to do with digestion. If you are distracted by bodily needs, this will obviously get in the way of the degree of concentration required to perform as a remote viewer. You should not try to do remote viewing immediately after consuming a large meal, especially a meal that contains a great deal of hard-to-digest material like meat, or acid-bearing foods. Being hungry doesn't help either. If you are thinking about the need to eat, or are bothered with a need to eat, then that should be taken care of at least an hour prior to remote viewing.

2. **Drugs.** I've been asked a lot about drugs. Some claim that certain kinds of drugs support the altered state that opens the doors to remote viewing information. Nothing could be further from the truth. Drugs suppress your abil-

ity to control what's going on in your mind. The art of remote viewing has much to do with the processing of the information and very little to do with reception, which is assumed to be taking place. Anything that gets in the way of being able to clearly understand and deal with how you might be processing information can only detract from the overall result. No good remote viewer that I know supports the use of any kind of drug. The idea is to learn to control what's happening, and drugs always have an adverse effect on that ability. Drugs are out.

3. **Sleep.** Some of us get along very well with seven hours of sleep at night. Some can get by on as little as five, or need as much as ten. This has to do with what you are habituated to. You should get as much sleep as you know you will need to eliminate the feeling of being tired. "Well-rested" is a phrase that comes to mind when thinking about what's necessary for viewing purposes.

4. **State of mind.** This is very difficult to control but is one of the most debilitating intrusions on good remote viewing. If you've just had an argument with someone, driven through bad traffic, feel pressured or hurried, or are not otherwise conducive to remote viewing, it will show in the results. A positive "can-do" attitude is essential to remote viewing success. Anything you can do to improve your state of mind is highly recommended. Ways to do that include having a set or recognized start time, something you can clearly begin to plan for, re-center your focus on. If you don't feel up for the remote viewing, postpone it until a better time. Only you can tell when you are up or down. You should do something that brings you pleasure an hour before viewing. This might be a hobby or other activity that relaxes you or refocuses your attention. It should be something that just keeps the mind busy, but doesn't over stimulate you. Develop a good attitude with regard to success or failure, by rewarding yourself in some way for being successful. I know viewers who do this by

only allowing themselves sweets after a successful remote viewing and at no other time. Finally, learn to deal with failure, after all, it's simply part of the learning process. Most of all, do not take yourself seriously. When you do, the fall from grace is much more painful. Retain your sense of humor.

5. **Control your ego.** When you are doing really well, your ego is well massaged. When you aren't doing so well, your ego will beat the heck out of you. In fact, ego is probably the most destructive element in all of the bad habits one might display as a viewer. It narrows your world. It's the engine that drives many of the nasty little personality traits that are destructive and get in the way of helping others. Without ego attachment to what you do, there is no greed or focus on the material. It's the harder road to follow, but the rewards as a viewer are far greater in the long run.

Things That Don't Seem to Support Remote Viewing

Aside from the above, other things that don't seem to support remote viewing include:

1. **A cluttered workspace.** If you are buried in clutter it will be reflected in your work. One must understand, however, that clutter to one person is protection and comfort to another. I know a very good writer whose office you almost can't get into, there are so many papers, books, and journals stacked about. This obviously brings a lot of comfort into his environment. So by clutter, I'm talking here about things that are distractions and non-supportive. Some believe that anything in the workspace introduces fantasy or overlay into the process. I do not believe this to be true. In my experience, feeling comfortable in your workspace is more important. Also, remember, anywhere you will have to use remote viewing in support of others

will be cluttered. Those are real world environments. Why teach yourself in an ideal situation, when you will have to operate in climates that are not ideal.

2. Interference. Turn off your phones, fax machines, and alarm clock, usher the cat out the front door, go to the bathroom before you start, and demand privacy while you remote view.

3. Tools. Make sure you have all the tools you will need before you start. The right kinds of pens and paper, a ruler if you need it, pencils, or whatever. Nothing is more irritating than to find you are missing something that is essential to the process.

4. Quiet. I'm not talking morgue quiet here, I'm talking reasonably quiet. There was a time when everyone believed that a soundproofed room was essential to viewing ability. This is probably wrong. It may be an excuse for failure when you are looking for one, but it isn't essential to remote viewing. You wouldn't want a pile driver or other heavy machinery operating just outside your window. In fact, the lack of sharp noises, repetitive noises, or irritating noises is probably a good idea. Remember, you are trying to encourage concentration. Some say this is a good reason for the soundproof room, but when you stop and think about it, you will realize that the world condition we consider normal is the common operating condition. I feel that making the conditions more optimal than can reasonably be expected is to set your self up for failure, as then almost any little distraction will interfere with the process.

Other Supportive Disciplines

Other things can support the mental control you are trying to establish. These range from the near impossible to what's generally achievable. Some of these are:

1. **Lucid Dreaming.** According to Stephen LaBerge, Ph.D., Stanford University Sleep Research Center, lucid dreaming is "being awake in your dreams." At one time or another everyone has probably experienced a lucid dream, that is, finding yourself living a dream which you suddenly recognize as being a dream. Maybe it's walking down the hall to the bathroom in the middle of the night, or working on that difficult project you've been trying to master. Right in the middle of the experience you realize, "Hey, I'm dreaming." Usually resulting in your waking up, but sometimes, it provides you the platform or the opportunity to be in control of what you are experiencing. Back in the mid-1980s, I participated in a number of experiments with Steven LaBerge in his sleep lab. I was tasked with creating a lucid dream, a state in which I knew I was asleep, but awake and dreaming. Once I realized I was lucid dreaming, it was my task to do a remote viewing of a randomly designated target. We were successful on a number of occasions. In fact, some of these successes were absolutely astounding. I believe that while the lucid dream state is difficult to initiate, difficult to maintain or use, it is quite conducive to remote viewing, and the discipline it takes to control such a state supports the kind of discipline required for viewing. (More information can be found about lucid dreaming in the book, *Lucid Dreaming, The Power of Being Awake & Aware in Your Dreams,* by Stephen LaBerge, Ph.D., J.P. Tarcher, Inc., Los Angeles, 1985 (Distributed By Houghton Mifflin Co., Boston, Massachusetts).

2. **Out of Body Travel.** Sometimes known as astral travel or traveling clairvoyance. This is the ability to actually re-locate to another place in every sense except physically. Sometimes this is confused with remote viewing. By comparison, the remote viewer sits in a room and describes their perceptions in relation to a target in another location. While s/he may accurately describe that other location, there is never any doubt that s/he is in the room where his or her body is located.

In the Out of Body Experience (OBE), people actually perceive that they have traveled to that location, and are present there in all ways except the presence of their physical bodies, which remain at their place of origin.

After my near-death experience in 1970, I had continuing spontaneous OBEs, but could not control them. In 1983, there was one man in the world who I felt I could trust who claimed he could control them, and that was Robert Monroe. He had been experiencing OBEs since 1958, and had demonstrated his control over these remarkable events. So, I attended a Gateway Voyage seminar at the Monroe Institute, Virginia, in the fall of 1983, after which I asked if he could help me. We worked together in his lab for a period of nearly fourteen months, where I was finally successful in learning to control the ability, albeit, not as well as he. We were able to visit a number of targets in both the Out of Body sense and through remote viewing.

While there are profound differences between these two methods, and a whole range of difficulties I will not go into here, I did find that there was substantial increase in control over my remote viewing ability as a result of the experience. You can find out more about OBEs by reading Monroe's classic book, *Journeys Out of the Body*, Doubleday and Co., 1971. If for no other reason than personal growth and insight, I strongly recommend a Gateway Voyage seminar. (Contact the Monroe Institute by writing 52 Roberts Mountain Road, Faber, Virginia 22938, or by phone: (804) 361-1500.)

3. **Relaxation.** This is different from what I term meditation, which is addressed as item number four. Relaxation is mental, as well as physical. People relax in different ways, depending upon their personalities. One of the best ways is through music. I'm not talking about music that is stimulating, like drums, rock, or heavy metal. I'm talking about softer types of music, oriented toward soothing the nerves or mood. Music can also be used in conjunction with other activities, which brings a restful feeling to the spirit, such as

yoga or Tai Chi, or almost any activity that brings a gentle and soothing feeling to the soul of the participant.

Some like to listen to music while working in the garden, or just sitting on a riverbank communing with nature. The idea is to slow down, become somewhat centered, and otherwise let the mind drift, or to become empty of disharmony, to become balanced. For many of us who seek refuge in such relaxation there are both mental as well as physical benefits. But, some will find that they are almost incapable of relaxation. They have to have something going on, some activity to occupy their mind. They are constantly on the move, agitated, or filled with anxiety. True relaxation is a difficult state to master. Mastering it will prove beneficial not only to remote viewing, but to your overall health and creativity. I've found that those who can master it do far better with remote viewing than those who cannot. If you can't spend "alone time" with yourself, how can you spend time with a remote viewing target? There are lots of books available on relaxation, but since each personality is different, you will have to find one that fits you best.

4. **Meditation.** The only definition of meditation that I would accept is that of Dr. Charles Tart, who states that it is "first of all a deep passivity, combined with awareness." You can find what he says about it in *Altered States of Consciousness,* edited by Charles Tart, Ph.D., Harper San Francisco, 1990. This is a compendium of knowledge that everyone should have on their bookshelf if they are at all serious about the paranormal.

When this book was published there were very few serious articles or publications available referencing meditation, at least scientifically. I'm happy to say there are now considerably more. The idea behind meditation is that when one sits passively and attempts to silence the inner fires of activity, deeper thoughts and resources become apparent and surface. All you have to do is change "deeper thoughts and resources" to "information" and you have a near perfect definition of the act of remote viewing. Physical relaxation plays a great deal in the ability to meditate, so if you haven't dealt with item three above, you need to go back to it before you involve yourself in the principles of meditation. One of the unique benefits of practiced meditation is the ability to deal with distractions. Those who have mastered a technique of meditation usually display an ability to deal quickly with a distraction, process it, then put it away while returning to the state of deeper thought.

Zen meditation, which is very popular, begins with a proper sitting position and controlled breathing. The idea is to reach an altered state of lucidity, where you lose all connection to your body and are able to bring a tremendous amount of concentration to a state of total detachment, or nothingness. Mystical and higher level religious experiences are known to occur while in this state. What it does to perception is the goal for the remote viewer, being able to observe and report to your own mind, without overlaying concepts or overlaying conclusions. I can tell you that your ability to meditate well will translate into more frequent successes when attempting remote viewing.

5. **Hypnosis.** Self-hypnosis is a way of bringing meditation and relaxation together. It's the ability to totally relax or separate oneself from the body (in combination with relaxation) and enter into an altered state (self-hypnosis) where the subconscious becomes more accessible. Interestingly, this combination actually opens someone to both verbal and non-verbal cueing—in short, neurolinguistic communications.

Neurolinguistic communication is the ability to pass information from one person to the other through the use of body, hand, leg, head, or facial movements or gestures. This can be done intentionally, such as expressions accompanying statements, or unintentionally through our habits that we are not consciously aware of, like shifting in the seat, or folding our arms across our chest.

Now should be the time you remember what I said about not having anyone in the room who knows anything about the target. Well, this is why. Time in a self-hypnotic state is the perfect time to train the subconscious through repetitive exercise. So, if you practice self-induced hypnotic states while you are practicing your remote viewing and correcting deficiencies in your viewing as you go, you will be entraining yourself to respond automatically to what is necessary to produce a positive or successful result. One of the best books available on the subject of hypnosis, and in particular self-hypnosis, is *Hypnosis, Questions & Answers,* B. Zilbergeld, M.G. Edelstien, and D.L. Araoz, editors, W.W. Norton Company, New York, 1986.

6. **Other things.** Two remaining areas of discussion are important, as they bring a lot to bear on the belief structure of the individual who is trying to be a good remote viewer. Both areas are pretty much ignored, at least in the Western World. They are theological beliefs and philosophical belief. If someone tells you they aren't important, walk away now, as s/he and you are playing with fire. Both are absolutely *essential* to remote viewing. Philosophical belief basically has to do with personal wisdom and the pursuit thereof. It is a search for a good understanding of reality that is more speculative than objective. It generally includes ethics, aesthetics, logic, metaphysics, and cognitive knowing. Theological belief, on the other hand, is mediated by one's belief in a god, a mystical source, a grand engineer, the source of all power, or, for some, a unifying theory that supports existence. In either case, where you position yourself philosophically or theologically determines your acceptance of how or why some things happen.

Think of that position as like balancing on a seesaw. The middle point, or fulcrum is considered the place of balance. That's where you want to be. If you are way off to one end, let's assume the right, you are probably not open enough to allow remote viewing to operate. If you are way off to the left, you are probably *too* open, too airy or flighty to deal with it. In one case (to the right), paranormal activity will increase your degree of anger and your disbelief. This directly affects both your *expectation* for success and your *intention* to experience it—both of which affect the outcome. In the other case (to the left), you will not be able to acknowledge the *body of rules* within which it must operate. You will be ignoring the protocols, and violating the basics tenets of truth within which it must reside in order to operate. Too much of either end of the seesaw will be destructive.

As one is exposed to remote viewing, it should move those somewhat to the right or left more towards the center or fulcrum point. Unfortunately, since philosophic and theological belief is almost never addressed (in fact it is generally ignored), it seems to drive people who are already right or left to their respective extremes. For me, this entire issue has always been a point or focus on ethics. It is the responsibility of those who introduce people to remote viewing (be they scientists, self-appointed instructors, anointed gurus, or an official government agency) to insure that proper guidance is provided with regard to philosophic or theological changes and appropriate roadmaps. In most cases they not only make no effort to address it in any way, they do not even know how, or acknowledge this responsibility.

Religious bias is inevitable, since no one is an exception in this regard. Even scientists who claim to be atheists are not excluded. Because someone claims not to believe in a god, one should not automatically assume they do not believe there is an order or rule by which things operate. In fact, most scientists that I know who claim to be atheistic do believe there are rules to how reality operates and in most cases they have dug their heels in a lot harder against paranormal phenomenon than those who have a religious bent. Religion can do some interesting things to what people are willing to accept as normal. Many individuals are openly hostile to remote viewing because some remote viewers refuse to acknowledge God as the eminent power behind their viewing ability. Some viewers ascribe their ability to God's power, which usually generates hostility from the other side of the fence. In all cases, what you believe does have an immediate effect on what boundaries you are willing to accept that might or might not mediate remote viewing ability. Because the theological reality of the viewer is never discussed, no one ever has a clear understanding for when the threshold of truth (what is actually known about remote viewing) and self-delusion (what is accepted without question) is crossed. This adds a substantial amount of variability to subjects who might be involved, or whether you are observing remote viewing taking place or something else entirely. In many cases, you end up with rules bent for religion's sake, where they would not be bent for other reasons.

As I've said previously, I ascribe to what would be considered a god by many, but a rule of order by others. In my view, God and the rules by which reality operate are one and the same. Saying you believe in one without acknowledging the other doesn't make any sense to me at all. What if science proves a religious tenet to be wrong? Well, then the religious tenet obviously needs to be changed. Where the discourse enters is obvious. We accept religious beliefs on faith, but accept science only by what it can irrefutably prove. The mistake is apparent. We cannot take such a position in either case. Human inter-pretation of religion is nearly always flawed, and assuming science is correct based on a temporary or immediate find-ing of the time, is inviting disaster because to do so, you must stray from the healthy view, or stop walking the skeptical middle-line.

I've been on the planet long enough to understand that

one person's philosophy is never going to be the same as another's. There may be points of commonality, but there will always be sufficient differences to generate argument. Philosophy itself is a "belief." At best, it is speculative and a pursuit of something that can never really be achieved—personal wisdom. The problem is that it decisively affects everyone's beliefs, concepts, and attitudes. It has a direct relation to every action we take, minor or major. We apply our own personal brand of philosophy to everything we do. It even affects our ethical values and judgments. Good and evil have an impact on personal philosophy, but only in equal importance. There is no rule that dictates one must be good in order to be philosophical. One can be considered evil and still operate philosophically.

There was certainly a philosophy behind Hitler's decision-making. We all have strengths and weaknesses that affect where we are philosophically. Some appear philosophically shallow in comparison to others. But don't be fooled. Personal philosophy runs deep, sometimes deeper than you can imagine. Prejudice is a foundation stone in someone's house of philosophic belief, as are personal values like right and wrong. Philosophic belief is the degree of energy behind anger, frustration with others, how far we are willing to bend backwards, or when we feel a need to fall on our sword; it's the underpinnings to our relationships, whether personal or professional. When someone is first exposed to remote viewing, where s/he is philosophically on that day and at that time, determines his or her baseline. All changes that occur from that point forward are built upon that baseline. With so many different philosophic foundations, it is not a surprise that each of us ends up with a totally different belief structure. It is impossible to design a philosophic outlook like we cut chocolate-chip cookies. But, at least we can insure the temperature is right and the cookies have been thoroughly cooked but not burned.

Instructions for Making and Using Dowsing Equipment While Remote Viewing

There are two kinds of dowsing equipment that are used while remote viewing. One is used in lieu of the Associative Remote Viewing (ARV) method for responding to binary type questions, like "YES" and "NO," "UP" and "DOWN," "FORWARD" and "BACKWARD," etc., and one is used for working with locations on a map. Either or a combination of both can be used to answer questions regarding location.

Since you just can't walk into most shops and buy dowsing equipment, there are ways of making your own, or using everyday implements instead.

The least complicated instrument is the pendulum. You can make a pendulum by tying almost any small weighted object to a short string or cord. I have found that the finer string or fishing line is best, and using a smaller but heavier weighted object does well, especially where there might be a breeze or wind.

Examples of what can be used as a weighted object are; a small fishing weight or sinker (fig 1a), a suitcase key (fig 1b), or almost anything pointed on one end and weighing more than the string.

(fig 1a)   **(fig 1b)**

I've included pictures of my own pendulum (figure 2a). It also has a small recess under the eye which you can fill with a small bit of whatever you might be looking for, such as gold, water, or threads from someone's clothing (fig 2b).

(fig 2a)   **(fig 2b)**

The idea is to hang the pendulum from a short string and then allow your subconscious to control the action of the pendulum while focusing on a specific question. For example, while you are using a map to look for where someone might have lost their ring, you would hold the pendulum directly over the map, moving it back and forth as it hangs from your fingers, all the while trying to hold the pendulum as still as possible. While you are doing that, you would be asking yourself, "Is the missing ring here?"

As the pendulum crosses areas of the map in which the ring is not located, it will produce a simple motion that will not change. It may be an up and down rocking or a left to right motion. The motion will always be different with each person. When you hit the place on the map in which the ring is located, it will suddenly change directions.

Since the motion the pendulum will take is always different for each person, and will even sometimes change with the same person, you should calibrate the pendulum before using it. A simple way to do that would be to hold the pendulum over a blank sheet of paper and simply state, "This is yes," and "This is no." The pendulum should react differently for each statement. Simply memorize which is which before you begin looking.

To demonstrate what I mean by this motion, let's assume we are looking directly down on the top of the pendulum while scanning a map. As you move the pendulum over the area of the map in which the object you are looking for is *not* located, it swings side-to-side (figure 1.) When you hit the location the object probably *is* located in, it changes direction and begins to swing up-and-down (figure 2.) Remember, direction of movement will be different for everyone.

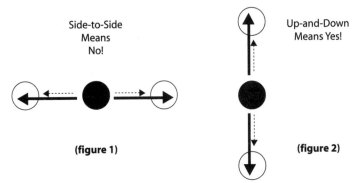

Side-to-Side
Means
No!

Up-and-Down
Means Yes!

(figure 1)

(figure 2)

"Side-to-Side Means No!" and "Up-and-Down Means Yes"

Another thing pendulums are good for is responding to questions. If you don't have time to set up an ARV protocol to pursue the binary answer to something, you can use your pendulum. Calibrate it the same way, then ask yourself the question to see what the pendulum does. Because binary questions are forced choice, I would only use the pendulum for this if I didn't have time to pursue an answer through the use of ARV.

Another simple tool that can be used for dowsing is a straight edge and pencil. These are used for determining a point on a map, grid, or diagram. The straight edge needs no markings on it to be used.

In order to find a specific point you need to define a horizontal and vertical line. Where they cross will be the point of interest.

To define the horizontal line, you simply place the straight edge at the bottom edge of the map or diagram horizontally, and push it upward with the left hand as you use the right hand to control the pendulum, all the while asking yourself the pertinent question.

As an example, beginning at the bottom (figure 1) you might be asking where is the best site for a potable water well site while pushing the straight edge up the center of

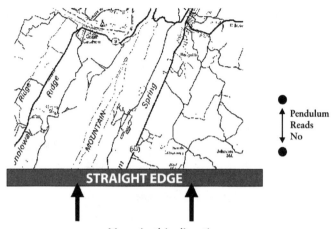

Pendulum
Reads
No

Move in this direction

(figure 1)

the map. Eventually getting a yes response on the pendulum, you then draw a horizontal line (figure 2).

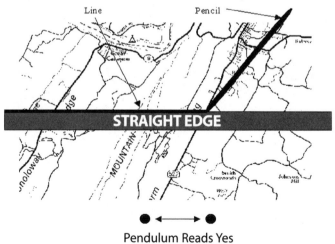

Pendulum Reads Yes

(figure 2)

You repeat the process for a vertical line (figure 3).

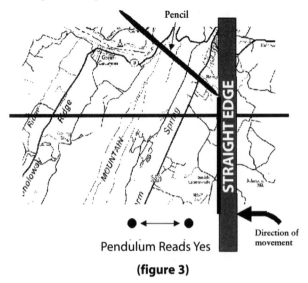

(figure 3)

Which provides you with a finished location (figure 4).

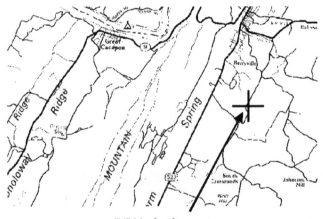

"X" Marks the spot

(figure 4)

Don't forget that you have to calibrate the yes and no answers with the pendulum before beginning.

There is a shortcut to the above method that does not require a pendulum. You simply give yourself a command to not blink your eyes unless the straight edge is directly over the correct site. It may take several passes, but practice will improve the results. You simply try not to blink while sliding the straight edge horizontally or vertically across the map. When you do blink, that is the point at which you should draw your line.

The blinking method can be used for occasions where you want to know something but don't want anyone to know you are dowsing. For example, while talking with a stranger you've never met, give yourself the command, "Blink when this person is lying." Or, while at a crime scene if you are wondering where to look for the most important evidence, you might scan the surroundings while at the same time giving yourself the command, "Blink when I'm looking in the right direction." You need to keep repeating the command in your mind while scanning. Let your subconscious direct you on when to blink.

Instructions for Building Equipment for Scrying

Scrying is another way of saying "crystal gazing." It is a way of divining distant, past, or future events based on visions seen in a polished-ball of rock crystal. Divination can also be done by staring at reflections on water or oil, or by peering into a polished metal surface. Early divination was done with round, polished metal surfaces in silver or gold, and by peering into the polished sides of precious stones. It has existed since around the fifth century but has historically been condemned by the Church as the work of the devil.

The way it works is a person usually stares directly into the crystal ball or reflective surface, concentrating for an extended period of time. Eventually, a sort of misting will begin to appear much like a cloud of fog. It's within this mist or fog, that visions are presented to the scryer. Of course you need to keep your specific question in mind while you are doing the staring.

It is strongly suggested that you write out your question before you begin and repeat it a number of times to yourself. Then once you begin, empty your mind of all thought. In order for the information to be presented, there needs to be a blank slate upon which to write.

Scrying usually takes a considerable period of staring when you are an initiate. But, over time, you will develop a talent for it, and the mist or fog will appear more rapidly. The lighting should be dim enough to not interfere, but bright enough that the inside of the crystal or bottom of the reflective pan can be seen through the water or oil medium. Some even use the light source itself as a scrying mechanism, such as a candle flame, or the smoke from a fire.

Expert scryers say the information really isn't in the medium of course. It lies within the mind of the individual. The fog or mist is actually created by the mind and occurs somewhere between the crystal ball and the scryer. It is actually a creative representation of reality within the individual's thought processes.

If scrying is done within the remote viewing protocol, then it is considered to be remote viewing. Surprisingly, some scryers have proven to be very effective in their information production, simply because they've mastered the ability to report only on what they see, without interpretation—the ultimate goal in any remote viewing effort.

Of course if you are interested in scrying, it is possible to purchase a crystal ball from your local new age supply shop. Unfortunately, they are usually grossly overpriced. Remember, it is not necessary for the crystal to be near flawless. In fact, the more fogging or interior flaws the better. It also doesn't have to be round. A crystal with a single polished side can be used. Also, it doesn't have to be crystal. It can be almost any kind of stone or glass that you can see into. The idea is to have a place to focus your attention to eliminate outside distractions.

If you would like to construct a divination tool very much like the one used by the Oracle of Delphi, it's really very easy.

You need to find a shallow dish with a bowl shaped bottom, and a mirrored surface. If you can't find one with a mirrored surface, you can create the mirrored surface by gluing a sheet of aluminum foil to the interior of the bowl (figure 1).

DIVINATION DEVICE

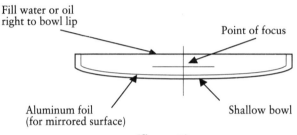

Fill water or oil
right to bowl lip

Point of focus

Aluminum foil
(for mirrored surface)

Shallow bowl

(figure 1)

The procedure is simple. Once you have written out your question, you need to relax and then stare directly into the fluid at the point-of-focus until a fog or mist begins to form. Once this begins to happen, you should search the fog or mist for a vision that will in some way be pertinent to your question. It will require a great deal of patience, since initially it will take some time before this will happen.

I will share one very important hint. As in any form of paranormal information gathering, do not automatically assume any vision presented is a literal representation of fact. In most cases, your subconscious will mask the real information.

If you lack a basic understanding of your own mental processing, or do not have at least a moderate under-standing for your own subconscious fears and desires, you will not be able to get to the core of what your mind presents.

Chapter Twelve

❋

Ethics

Ethics not only addresses what's good and bad, it encompasses a moral duty and obligation. This means that it is not only personal, but something we owe to others. In other words, they shouldn't have to come and ask us for it.

As an individual, ethics should be the backbone of our personal philosophy of living. Many get into trouble in determining the range or boundaries of ethical behavior. Most think of ethical behavior as determined by governmental laws, but this is only partially true. It is more a philosophically generated standard that is developed and pursued by individuals or sometimes groups. Which means that sometimes, part of your ethical standards may not be written down and may not originate from what is considered good or bad solely by your government. It may also come from what you learned from your parents, teachers, minister, or what you picked up from a peer group. Since we are all culturally and socially quite different, it is easy to see that ethical differences exist. For one, the ethics of invading someone's personal life or feelings would be abhorrent. For another, it would be a gift of kindness. Background, experience, culture, personal philosophy and even theological belief usually come into play, when it comes to ethics.

So, how would one distinguish a proper ethical standard, from an improper one?

This I can only suggest. Being American, I favor at least starting with the personal rights and freedoms our forefathers guaranteed us with the Constitution. The right to personal privacy and protection of that privacy are high on the list. I also like the idea that one human being will not do anything that damages or harms others, or in any way infringes on their rights to be who and what they want to be (as long as they too are not hurting others). Already we can see that for ethics to work, everyone has to have them, and the key seems to fall somewhere within the subject area of doing no harm. So, all ethical behavior should be positive and constructive and not negative or destructive.

It doesn't take a rocket scientist to see that world history is rife with examples of governments and social structures proclaiming certain actions as ethical which we see as not so. Numerous and explicit acts of racism and religious intolerance have been built on the foundations of faulty ethical belief or behavior. In some cases millions of people accepted certain behaviors as appropriate that came at the expense of other human beings. Or, at least that was always the argument at the time. But, I believe that even then, people knew they were being ethically wrong.

Today, there are gangs in many of our larger cities who follow what they believe to be a "code of ethics." But in these cases, as throughout history, this really isn't ethics we are talking about.

These situations occur because people sometimes look to others for guidelines upon which to base their ethical behavior. In almost every case, they do this because it is easier than taking a stand against what they know in their hearts is wrong from the outset. True ethics is a matter of the heart. It is acknowledging that for every action we take, we are in some way affecting others, and this includes the environment, non-human life-forms; essentially everything we have to live in harmony with on the planet. Or if you subscribe to the idea, even entities we know nothing about whom live in the stars as well.

There is a belief that since no one ever knows when or where a remote viewer or psychic penetrates reality, there are no ethical reasons why they shouldn't. This is clearly wrong. To begin with, the laws regarding a person's privacy do exist with regard to a telephone tap or poking through their private files. To assume it's okay to invade someone's privacy because it's telepathy and not yet specifically defined within the law is splitting hairs. While it may be awhile before the courts decide what to do about telepathy, it doesn't negate anyone's personal responsibility for upholding what was ethically intended by the Constitution. Even my editor suggested that until a law is written, the best anyone can do is "sympathize." I disagree. The least that anyone should do is acknowledge the intent and spirit of the law, and then follow it.

The following are not intended to be "ethical rules of behavior" for remote viewers or psychics, but is suggested as perhaps a line of minimal behavior, or at least a starting point for discussion.

Privacy

I would suggest that when it comes to remote viewing or psychic behavior, the same rules of privacy exist regarding individuals as do in any other case. It is unethical to pry, look, invade, or otherwise violate the personal privacy of an individual except at times and in ways allowed by law.

If parents come to me and ask that I find their son or daughter, and the son or daughter is over the age of consent, I can do only what the parent would ask a private detective or policeman to do: try to locate the son or daughter, and then attempt to deliver a message of concern from the parents to them. I cannot give the location to the parents directly, as that would be a violation of the son or daughter's privacy. Maybe the son or daughter doesn't want to be found.

Of course for every case there are exceptions. Perhaps there is reason to believe the son or daughter is in trouble, or is suffering from mental defect, whatever. These are always ethical judgment calls, or minefields. However you might view them, the rights of the individual must be held above all other factors.

Criminals have rights as well. However, things really begin to get sticky here. If invading the home of a criminal helps the law locate them, is that ethical? There is no warrant. To my knowledge, this has not yet been addressed by the courts, but clearly it should be. Most psychics attempt to provide clues external to the criminal's home or automobile, something that can be seen by the general public anyway, as pointers to location. What about a criminal's motivation?

I don't think a remote viewer or psychic does anything more than what a very good criminal profiler does— provide a best guess based on perceived and otherwise disconnected detail(s).

What about ideas?

We live in a world where more and more, ideas are considered of extreme value. New chemical blends, metal-lurgical processes (especially in the computer or electronic-chip business, where a process that reduces the insulator by a micron has meaning), even fashion statements, drive huge profits. We are talking now about the idea stage, where creativity is taking place. What about the ethics of stealing such a property?

My view is that the dividing line here is unclear. First, I automatically assume all creative processes to be nothing more than remote viewing or psychic functioning in any event. (Remember how I suggested that we eventually know the answer anyway, and it is then perhaps that we send it to ourselves in the past?) It seems to me that if we eventually know about something because it will eventually come into existence, it is not surprising that we might pick up on it in some psychic fashion before it actually does. There is already clear evidence that most new things popping out of the woodwork are quickly followed by like products. There is a tendency to believe the similarities are too synchronistic to have been independently created, but I think that would be an incorrect assumption. Knowing what I do about remote viewing, I would rather believe that ideas, like plants, do suddenly propagate in multiple greenhouses. So, the dividing line lies somewhere between the idea and the actual creation. If we can't tell where that line actually lies, we have to look for another indicator to answer our ethical dilemma, which in my opinion would be the motivation behind those pursuing the new product.

Targeting an individual or a company in order to collect ideas that you can use first is not ethically or morally responsible. Some hair-splitters would say, "Hey, if they want to lay claim to an idea, they have to bring it out first. We're just cutting it off at the pass." Sorry, but in my own opinion that's still industrial espionage. If your original intent or motivation is to "steal" or "pick up" the idea someone else is already working on, then you are ethically deficient.

In America, industrial espionage is considered illegal. Advertising to use remote viewing in industrial espionage should be punishable under the same laws that are currently in effect regarding other forms of industrial theft, or breaking and entering.

It is clear that some psychics want to have their cake and ice cream too. They operate under the idea that "since officially no one wants to admit that remote viewing or psychic functioning is real or that it works, they can hardly take me to court and charge me with theft using it. On the other hand, if they take me to court and are able to prove it's real, they've essentially bolstered my claims about what I can do with it, which equals more business at a higher price." It becomes a kind of win/win for the psychic.

However, from both a moral and an ethical viewpoint, the psychic or remote viewer who takes that position is clearly in the wrong.

If on the other hand, your motivation is simply profit and you are looking for input in support of an idea you might have and use a remote viewer to get it—out of the ethers, if you will—then so be it. It will have to be a patent attorney's issue if an argument arises. No one acknowledges where ideas come from. I suspect that the origin of ideas is actually within the person's head who conceives them. Whether using remote viewing or just thinking really isn't material. If you truly understand remote viewing or psychic functioning, you understand it's all pretty much one and the same thing.

Profit, Greed, and Ego

Many believe that psychic ability and remote viewing are gifts from God and therefore should not be used for profit, in support of greed and or personal aggrandizement. If you attempt to use it in this way, it won't work, or you will fail. I've got some sad news for you, if you believe this is true. Unfortunately, it's not.

I have seen absolutely no evidence that a person's morality or ethical behavior mediates talent in any way. There are certainly lots of reasons why such attitudes might get in the way, but in my opinion these are technical issues and have nothing to do with the person involved. A morally corrupt person can be just as good at it as someone who isn't.

I think this belief is actually born out of a hope and

desire that it might be so. Many of us are taught that when people do bad things they get caught and suffer for it. Perhaps, psychologically, since some people can see no way that someone might be held responsible for their actions as a psychic or remote viewer, except in the eyes of God, they have trouble imagining why God would allow them to use it for evil or bad things.

Sometimes, the very act of being psychic is viewed as the work of the devil. After all, if it's "god-like knowing," and only God can have that, then it just has to be devil-inspired. All of these views, of course, are driven by religious fervor or fanaticism, dependent upon your point of view.

In my own point of view, the ability to be psychic or do remote viewing is purely based on innate talent, the amount of exercise or practice you've had doing it during your lifetime, and the appropriate application of technique and protocol—none of which have anything at all to do with a person's ethics. The ethics part we are obligated to apply ourselves.

Technically, many of these things can be perceived as pertinent to effective viewing, simply because they drive the belief system of the people participating in the act. Once you understand that, the mystery surrounding evil people, out-of-control egos, and how they might affect psychic performance vaporizes rather quickly.

Other Ethics in Remote Viewing

Other ethical questions surrounding the subject of remote viewing, are even less clear-cut. They have to do with "when" information should be used.

In the past, I have spoken about times when it became known to some of my colleagues that I was not always sharing all of the information I might have collected during a remote viewing. This sometimes happens, even when there is no obvious ethical constraint. Why would I not share information, especially when asked to do so by the very people it will be affecting?

The answer will not be a surprise to some. As a remote viewer with twenty-one-years experience, I know in many cases, as good as I might feel about the information I might be perceiving, there is no way for me to know ahead of time that it is absolutely real or accurate.

Remember, being psychic is a double-edged sword. I not only get information of interest, but I usually have some perception of why the information is needed, even when I'm not being told. Therefore, if I perceive that an action will be taken that could ultimately harm someone because the information could be wrong, I just don't provide it.

Lets say I produce information that implies that someone has done something wrong. But, I also know that even a subsequent investigation, which may prove them innocent, will not undo what has been implied, I do not provide the information. A good example would be feeling that I have sufficient information from remote viewing to indicate that someone is a child molester. Unless there was already a substantial amount of information available through other sources that indicated the same, or I had absolute trust that authorities would not use the remote viewing information as sole source information, I would not report the information. In our society, just the accusation of something like that can be devastating to another human being. Knowing what I know about remote viewing, it would be the last information I would depend on for making such an accusation. So there are times, regardless of input, when you should just shut up and sit quietly.

Of course, if you've been paying attention, you should be thinking that no one should ever be using remote viewing information as sole source for anything anyway. But, in my experience, when it comes to the pursuit of crime, they are likely to use the viewing information as stand-alone information, usually to generate new leads. This may be okay if it opens new avenues of information that can be approached with conventional law enforcement techniques—and as long as it doesn't harm another human being.

Another example of bad ethical practices is "Psychic Hot Lines." I know this probably ruffles a lot of feathers, but hear me out.

I'm sure there are a number of very good psychics who participate very ethically through psychic hot lines. However, that is not the reason for which they have been created. You need to look at the fine print. Psychic hot lines are set up for entertainment purposes. They are not set up to give critical and accurate advice to people who are hurting, looking for their next job, or otherwise in dire need of serious assistance. Those who say they are, are deluding themselves. There are lots of examples of unethical statements surrounding psychic hot lines, probably too many. "He's/she's cheating on you." "Your emotional body map is setting you up for a serious illness." "You need to sell your house and move." These kinds of statements, whether the psychic believes them to be true or not, are unconscionable. The best-of-the-best in the psychic world has nowhere near the kind of accuracy that would be required to advise someone blindly to sell a house or cut off a relationship.

What about *serious* psychics and remote viewers? I'm a very serious remote viewer and I would never give that kind of advice to anyone for any reason. In this business, you need to assume that the very reason someone is asking you something, is because they take you seriously in the first place. It is an awesome responsibility that should not be taken lightly. A great deal of time and thought should go into the ethical lines you draw around yourself as a remote viewer or psychic. If they are drawn properly, you are choosing not to share, more than you are sharing.

One last comment is necessary regarding ethical behavior.

In remote viewing training, there are many training techniques that do not focus on the philosophical or theological impact to the viewer. Since belief has such a strong effect on the outcome of such training, and conversely, training has such a strong effect on belief, not addressing this impact, or not paying attention to the changes taking place in the student, in effect letting the student fend for him or herself, is, in my opinion, unethical behavior.

Ethics That Affect Remote Viewing

A number of other areas have a direct affect on remote viewing and need to be talked about, at least in terms of ethics and/or ethical behavior.

Media.
Project STARGATE was terminated in November 1995. Since then, I've had interaction with dozens of television production companies, a number of newspaper, magazine, and book writers, and live and taped radio show hosts. I would like to say that all of them have been ethical in how they approached the serious subject matter, or me, or others connected with remote viewing or its research. In fact, few have.

Many of the programs looking for film footage were only loosely disguised as news programming, when their very existence is for entertainment purposes only. In some cases, they did everything possible to sensationalize or trivialize the truth to make a better story.

Some companies that were news-oriented spent little time seeking out a proper balance when presenting the facts; instead, they went with whomever they could get to show themselves on camera, regardless of their level of interest, degree of expertise, or previous connection to the subject matter.

Many in the media automatically assumed an attitude

of ridicule long before they did their first interviews, took their first foot of film, or asked their first interview question.

It is not surprising to me that many in America, or elsewhere for that matter, do not know what appropriate ethics are. This may sound like harsher criticism than is warranted, but it isn't. In my experience, those who were clearly operating from high ethical standards were the smaller percentage. At least there were enough of them to inspire hope for the industry.

Internet.

In America, everyone who has the money to buy a computer can gain access to the Internet. The number of Internet users in America alone has topped twenty-three million. However, one should remember that the second leading country is Canada with a mere 1.75 million Internet users.

On the surface this sounds great. Well, have I got news for you: the Internet system is the greatest source of disinformation available to the public today.

There are essentially no rules for operating on the Internet. Outside of sale or advertising of medicines or other controlled substances, over the net, you can pretty much say whatever you would like to say, as you are protected by your right to free speech. The Internet is just like putting up a soapbox in the park.

There is nothing wrong with that, except that a lot of people operating over the Internet have absolutely no ethical standards. Claims and statements are made which have no basis in fact. They are designed specifically for a lot of reasons, but truth is not one of them.

Obviously, nothing is going to be done in the near future to correct this problem, and maybe there shouldn't be. So, I would strongly suggest that if you seek out facts or truth regarding remote viewing on the Internet, accept whatever you find with a large grain of salt, or go to the trouble to verify it. Taking information directly off the net and attempting to use it will only add to the confusion.

Chapter Thirteen

✳

Recommendations About Training

For twenty-one years I've been saying the same thing about training—you can't teach someone to be psychic.

Unfortunately, this has been interpreted a lot of different ways, most of which have been out of context, and in many cases with ill intent—to discredit in some way. When I say this, I'm usually saying it within the context of the question.

"Can I learn to do that?"

The "that" which is being implied, pertains to a specific example of remote viewing just seen—what I would call a world-class result.

Of course the percentage of what I would call world-class remote viewing is very small, or at least it has been with me. "Successful" has always been a relative term. Statistically, I can say emphatically that almost all scientists who have studied remote viewing would generally agree that even after training of some sort, the number of world-class remote viewers (world-class in this case means viewers who can systematically and consistently defy chance results in controlled studies in a lab) probably comes in at around one-half of one percent of any randomly tested group of people, or about one person in two hundred.

I think the confusion comes in somewhere between that reality and the fact that just about everyone who's ever walked into a lab and been tested shows some degree of remote viewing ability, a seemingly contradictory statement.

In fact, both statements are true. Putting them together should read: "Anyone can remote view; only about one-half of one percent can do it really well." Does training make a difference between just being able to do it and doing it really well? Yes, probably some, but not enough that it's going to push you from one end of the scale to the other.

This is actually very encouraging news. It means that there isn't anything about remote viewing that you can't get with a reasonable amount of effort and diligence, and you can probably get it from just about anyone who follows protocol and encourages you to practice, even if it's only yourself doing the encouraging. There are no secrets beyond most of those shared between these covers. You will also be able to tell if you are going to be any good at it from the outset.

I know this news will be discomforting to some because they might have been led to believe something different, but those are the facts, at least as I understand them.

I have always strongly recommended that when it comes to training or learning about remote viewing, you should set your own course and proceed with vigor. I've suggested there really is no great mystery in mastering it, as it requires practice more than anything else. Since it's predominantly talent-driven, much like athletic or musical ability, it will demand training from the standpoint of repetition more than anything else. In other words, follow the protocols and practice, practice, practice.

Aside from this book, other sources of material directly relate to the learning of remote viewing. Some of these relate directly and some relate less directly. There are also goals that you can reasonably expect to attain as well as goals that most will probably never attain. I can suggest how you might be able to judge your progress, and, quite frankly, when you should probably quit.

Of course you don't have to believe any of this, but you can expect to save a lot of money, effort, and time if you do. The thing to remember is that you alone can judge the effectiveness of what you are doing, and only you can determine when you've given enough in terms of effort, money, or time. Remember: think of remote viewing as a martial art. It is a way of, and not an end unto itself.

Reasonable Expectations

For almost anyone who has no previous knowledge about remote viewing, some reasonable expectations can be stated about learning it. Where you fall in relation to these expectations is solely dependent on whatever innate talent you possess when you walk through the door. No one can have a clue as to the level of talent someone might possess prior to actually testing it, but like athletes, it doesn't take much to tell whether or not you will do well with a specific sport or activity. One of the nice things about it is, it isn't like basketball or football. Size doesn't matter, and even if you aren't a superstar, you can have fun with it.

Almost without exception, anyone first exposed to remote viewing will be able to generate what are considered major gestalts. This means that once they understand what is expected of them, they should, from time-to-time, be able to tell the differences between islands, mountains, deserts, cities, or other major geographic features. Initially they will be able to do this about twenty-five percent of the time. Those who seem to be good at it—have demonstrable talent—will probably increase their ability to about fifty percent after sufficient exposure and practice. It's impossible to estimate how much time it will take anyone to get to the fifty-percentile point since each person will have differing degrees of focus, participation, and practice. But, I would plan on months.

During that period of time, bits and pieces of other stages are possible, and will be reflected in the results. You should bear in mind that sporadic reflections of more detail about specific targets does not necessarily guarantee someone has a great deal of inherent talent. The majority of people exposed to remote viewing will produce more sophisticated fragments of information about a target such as sensory values like touch, taste, sound, color, as well as dimensional characteristics, mental perceptions or feelings about the site. The average person may even provide statements about a specific object or function at the target location.

What's nice about this is that this is what almost anyone can do coming out of the starting gate. Misconceptions center on how often or how dependably someone can provide the more sophisticated forms of data. This kind of detail doesn't happen very often with the average person, and believe me, it won't be very dependable either.

Many are currently being exposed to remote viewing through training systems that underscore this level of achievement and provide a framework in which it can be displayed. The problem is, this is about as good as most will ever get. I receive dozens of phone calls now on a week-to-week basis from people asking me what they are doing wrong. They've taken one training course or another but can't seem to settle down into a high quality or consistent viewing product. Well, guess what? You're in the 95th percentile of any randomly selected group of humans.

Most training systems will provide a framework inside of which the information can be broken down into categories that are recognizable—from the easily recognized major gestalt to the more sophisticated details about a target such as specific objects, descriptions, or assessments. These training systems may even provide a disciplined approach to recognizing how and when certain levels of input are being processed. But, the degree of detail the target can be broken down into, the accuracy and consistency in which it can be reported, or the refinement one brings to the task is purely dependent on the person's innate talent, that is the perceptive skills brought to the table.

For those who fall in the one-half of one percent and have a great deal of talent, the training can be helpful in showing you how to break down the material as you are receiving it. To a certain extent, some forms of training will even provide a disciplined approach to how you might process the stuff coming into your head. However, you can look forward to a long and difficult road if you intend to master remote viewing. Because you are talented, you will have more hits in the "specifics or details" about targets, but you can also expect two things. First, attaining consistency and reliability will be a lifelong battle you will have to fight on a day-to-day, target-by-target basis. It's something you can never relax with. Second, aside from consistency and reliability, your ability will probably not improve, no matter what you do. Over the course of their careers, every exceptional viewer studied in the cognitive sciences labs at SRI-International (SRI-I) and Science Applications International Corporation (SAIC) have essentially produced a near flat-line in terms of ability. Independent surges and spikes of success appear now and then during a focused or narrow parameter study, but over all—that is, statistically—the best remote viewers don't change. They are as good walking in the door as they are when they exit.

Setting Up Your Own Training Schedule

There is no magic in setting up your own training schedule and arranging your own pool of targets, but for some reason I get letters from people all the time asking me if I know where they can plug into a target pool, or participate in remote viewing exercises. It's a simple process to explain, but terribly difficult to actually sit down and do. Or, even more importantly, to forget once you've done it.

The problem actually has more to do with what goes on in the mind after the target pool has been set up. Most people find they can't help but remember many of the targets they put in the pool when they were building it. So, when it comes time to do the remote viewing, their minds are flooded with snapshots of many of the targets they know are in the pool. Even randomly pulling a target from a pool with a hundred possibilities doesn't seem to help. The mind still has a tendency to fill with all those wonderful snapshots and all those things you thought about while you were selectively building the pool.

The only way around this is to have others build the pool for you and then not let them tell you anything about it. Assuming they follow the recommendations I set out earlier about what makes a good training target, you can reduce their load by telling them to only make four or five targets at a time. Since others are actually building it for you, and you are blind to what they have selected, the pool doesn't have to be very large. If you have no one to help you, then you are pretty much stuck with building a substantial pool or possibly finding someone over the Internet or through the mail who might be willing to share a pool with you.

Some people wonder why some of us remote viewers do not share our target pools with others. It's because it takes a considerable amount of time and effort to construct a good pool of practice targets. I've been building my target pool that I use for practice for about ten years. Most of the targets I've selected I have either photographed myself, or have obtained by looking through thousands of copyright-free photographs available through commercial sources. Most of these photographs have been cropped appropriately, extraneous materials excised, etc. I've even gone to the extent of erasing people and non-connected objects from the foreground so as not to have any distractions. I take the practice pool very seriously. This should give a very large hint about how seriously you should take making one for yourself. If you are serious about teaching yourself something, you should be willing to spend the appropriate amount of energy and effort to collect the right tools. *The primary tool for a remote viewer is the practice pool.*

Next in importance is making sure you have set aside a very specific time and place in which to do your practice session. Minimal requirements are:

1. Use the same place every time if possible, at least during training.

2. Try to fix a specific time that stays constant. If you are a working person, maybe this will be 7:00 A.M. or 9:00 P.M. on a Tuesday or Thursday, either just before you leave for work (if you're a morning person), or after you've gotten home and finished dinner or the rest of your errands. It could also be on weekends if you can't turn your job off after coming home. Those who are retired or otherwise can plan a time in the middle of the day. It should center on a period when you know you have good energy and nothing will interrupt what you are doing.

3. Turn off the phone, usher the cat and dog outside, put a cover over the bird, close the door and hang up a "do not disturb" sign. Your mind needs to be centered and focused for learning.

4. Keep a notebook and use it for everything you don't want to forget or that might seem important to you. Remember: if you think it, it's important.

5. Pay particular attention to details. You should be able to differentiate between the kinds of informa-

tion you are processing: gestalts, sights, sounds, feelings, tastes, colors, dimensions, perceptions, details, actions, assessments, and conclusions. Try to focus on the ones that you don't seem to do very well with. Assume that the ones you do get routinely will take care of themselves.

6. Work at it for no more than fifteen minutes. Whatever you get in fifteen minutes is probably all you're going to get, initially. Later, when you can demonstrate an ability to get the major gestalts in a fairly consistent manner, extend the time to take into consideration other more detailed elements that might be pertinent to the target.

7. Always choose your target randomly and always work it as a blind target. (I've already stated all the reasons why this is necessary.)

Most of you will find that you can do a very good job with the overall gestalt for the target, but will consistently have difficulty with the details. For some reason you will not be able to hit those except every now and then. That's okay. Welcome to the 95th percentile. If you can do reasonably well with consistency on major target gestalts, with a few details about color or target dimension thrown in now and then, regardless of what anyone tells you, you are doing about as well as it's going to get.

How to Judge Your Own Results

This is where it's a lot more fun to be working with others: You have someone to share your "hits" with. That can be very exciting and helps to give you the drive to continue. When you work alone, it is a lot more difficult maintaining the momentum.

The results actually speak for themselves. What you find in most cases are very recognizable plateaus. These are like resting places, where after you get so much improvement, you find yourself suddenly stuck. Don't worry about it. It's normal and natural. These can last for weeks or months. It will mean one of two things:

1. You have reached your level of natural talent, in which case you can continue to try to increase your consistency and dependability at that level. Like most things in RV, this is not a fixed rule. Sometimes, after a long drought in progress, you will suddenly see a marked improvement. It will be as though a logjam has somehow unlocked up stream. If that happens, great, then you are at. . .

2. . . . a real plateau, and eventually you will move on to the next one. You never know ahead of time just how many plateaus you might encounter, where your level of talent might take you, or how long it will take to get there. It's always a surprise. Beware of training systems that give you a guarantee. If they say they can guarantee that you will be proficient at a specific level above the general gestalt, I would question it.

Knowing When to Quit

This is probably the easiest question to answer. You quit when you aren't having any fun anymore. Remote viewing should be fun, even when you aren't learning anything. It's fun to meet with others who enjoy it, it's fun to be with others who practice it, and it's fun to try using it in training and applications. If you are becoming frustrated, angry, depressed, worried, upset, anxious, or having any other unsettling feelings about it, then it's time to quit. If you find yourself arguing with others about what you are doing, it's time to quit. If you fear failure, it's time to quit. If you can't be satisfied with the degree of gift you were given walking in the door, it's time to quit.

One of the prime bits of information you should have gotten from this book is the knowledge that everyone operates at a different capacity and at a different level. You can polish your understanding of remote viewing to a degree that you can truly master whatever level of remote viewing you personally operate at. Even operating at the major gestalt level can bring you information you never dreamed of. Employed in a creative sense, it can open doors previously closed to you. When you start fighting yourself over it, you will only be doing damage.

Since I do not teach remote viewing myself, I've been asked many times over the years to recommend someone who does. I recommend you teach yourself. I sincerely believe that this is appropriate because I believe that individual perception is more a matter of unlearning than learning. The name of the game is discovering your own bad habits, at least in regard to internal processing, and eradicating them. Learning how to do this from someone else can only make that process more difficult. You pick up new habits along the way.

Now, having said that, if you still need someone to guide you along the path, there are two recommendations I would make, contact information for both can be found on the Internet.

1. Paul Smith. Remote Viewing Instructional Services (RVIS)

2. Lyn Buchanan. Problems, Solutions, and Innovations (PSI)

Neither recommendation should be viewed as a judgment about any other training facility, office, business, or person. Nor should it be construed to mean there are no others. I only recommend these two because I am familiar with both of them personally, I have a clearer understanding for how and why they train in a specific way, and I know they are open to change, improvement, and continued learning in the field of remote viewing, or at least hope they are.

When it comes to the science of remote viewing, I would recommend trusting absolutely no information that does not originate from a recognized scientific laboratory or spring from a peer-reviewed and appropriately refereed journal. So far, absolutely no evidence suggests that what can be learned about remote viewing requires changing the basic rules of science.

Appendix A

Glossary of Terms

There are a lot of terms associated with remote viewing that have developed over the years. Keeping track of them is very difficult sometimes. Some of the terms can be misleading, like "Remote Viewing" itself, which implies actually seeing a target when you may not see anything at all. To assist you in understanding, I've included this list of remote viewing terms, which are my own perceptions as to what the different terms means.

I've used the term "hypothetically" many times within this list of definitions of terms. The terms I've used it with are those where there has been an assumption made and truth has not been established regarding that term or definition. In other words, just because one assumes something is true, doesn't make it automatically true.

AESTHETIC IMPACT (AI): A dramatically sudden and spontaneous opening to information about a target.

ANOMALOUS COGNITION (AC): Term used by the Cognitive Sciences Laboratory to define Extra Sensory Perception (ESP).

APPLICATION: A remote viewing application is the production of information through the use of a technique or method that is based on a tested protocol.

ANALYTIC OVERLAY (AOL): A subjective observation of

incoming information made by the remote viewer that may or may not be relevant to the actual target or its content.

APERTURE: Viewpoint of the remote viewer that hypothetically indicates a broad to narrow orientation of perception to the target and/or its details.

ASSOCIATIVE REMOTE VIEWING (ARV): Using a targeting methodology which allows the remote viewer to operate one level removed from the actual target, in order to address forced choice type questions (yes/no, go/stop, invest/don't invest, etc.).

ASSUMPTION: A conclusion based on insufficient or incomplete information. Assumptions are nearly always wrong in part or whole.

BLIND TARGETING: Focusing the remote viewer on a target which the remote viewer is totally blind to, and for which there is no front-loading, or other preparation. (Note: this includes anyone else participating in the remote viewing being blind to the target as well, otherwise the remote viewer is not considered to be actually blind to the target).

CENTERED: Point or place of balance within one's thoughts. In a Zen sense, a place of no thought or empty thought.

COLD READING: Direct interaction between a psychic and an individual, where the psychic determines information pertinent to the individual through means other than paranormal (e.g., by reading body reactions—neurolinguistics).

CONCLUSION: A reasoned judgment. Unfortunately, sometimes based on inaccurate or incomplete assumptions.

CONSCIOUS (Mind): A perception or observation that is recognized and experienced. An accepted knowing whether true or not, that anchors us to the material world and experience.

COORDINATE REMOTE VIEWING (CRV): Form of remote viewing used by remote viewers many years ago, which entailed prompting the remote viewer with specific geographic coordinates for a specific target site.

COORDINATE: Any alpha/numeric set used to distinguish the identity of one target from another. (Note: does not necessarily imply geographic location.)

DEBUNKER: Generally a closed minded individual who attacks what they do not understand or fear, usually under the guise of skepticism, or with the intention of proving fraud even when fraud may not exist.

EGO: Organized part of one's consciousness that attempts to control what will be accepted as real, as a result of the interaction between one's perception and what one believes to be reality.

EMOTIONAL IMPACT: A sudden or spontaneous perception of human emotional content pertinent to the target.

FEEDBACK: Correct target responses given to the viewer after the remote viewing session has been terminated and the target will not be revisited.

FREE RESPONSE: Generally refers to data provided by subjects participating in remote viewing or ganzfeld experiments, where the subject's response is not controlled but allowed to occur spontaneously.

GESTALT: An overall or gross perception of a target that may contain a significant sense of what the target is, contain patterns, or other commonalities prevalent within the target, but provides insufficient elements to permit an otherwise greater determination about the target.

IDEOGRAM: A reflexive mark on a paper, hypothetically made as a result of the impingement of a signal line on a person's autonomic nervous system. (Note: This is an essential element of belief or underpinning to the CRV method of Remote Viewing).

MEDITATION: Mental contemplation or reflection with an intended purpose or expected outcome.

METHOD: A method (methodology), is a systematic procedure or mode of inquiry employed by, or proper to, a particular discipline or art. In remote viewing, these are always applied within the framework of a protocol.

MONITOR: Person who assists the viewer in a remote viewing session. The monitor provides the viewer with appropriate targeting material, records remote viewing session information, and assists the viewer in staying within the bounds of protocol. (Note: Monitor is always as blind to the target as the viewer should be.)

NOISE: Various forms of overlay that are perceived as possibly interfering with the information being processed by the remote viewer.

OPERATIONAL RV: This would be a remote viewing directly applied as an application, and otherwise not used for practice, demonstration, or scientific study.

OUTBOUNDER: Person who acts as a target beacon while visiting a target location during a remote viewing session. (Note: This hypothetically gets the remote viewer to focus on the specific target site of interest.)

PERCEPTIONS: Information about the target which the remote viewer acquires that may or may not be correct about the target.

PRECOGNITION: Producing information about a target prior to that information actually existing in time/space (e.g., describing an event before it actually happens).

PROTOCOL: A remote viewing protocol is a detailed plan of a scientific experiment, treatment, or procedure. It is the first step in the design of an application.

PSYCHIC: A person who is sensitive to perceptions or understanding that is not available through ordinary means.

PSYCHIC FUNCTIONING: The collection and production of information without the use of the physical senses.

REMOTE VIEWER: Person who can demonstrate the acquisition of information through the use of remote viewing while operating under appropriate scientific controls.

REMOTE VIEWING: The ability to access and provide accurate information through psychic means, about a person, place, object, or event, that is inaccessible through any normally accepted means, regardless of distance, shielding, or time. (Note: The term was originally coined by researchers at SRI-International in the early 1970s.)

REMOTE VIEWING SESSION (FORMAL): Specific period of time during which an actual remote viewing takes place. Should always have a noted start time, and viewer should be told specifically when that will be ahead of time if possible.

Also has a specific stop time, after which all records are sealed and no one adds any further information to the remote viewing data.

REMOTE VIEWING SESSION (INFORMAL): This can be a practice session or other remote viewing that is totally controlled by the remote viewer in terms of time. While the start/termination time can be open, and up to the viewer, the viewer should have no feedback or knowledge of the target until the session has been formally terminated.

RV'DO: The way of Remote Viewing, or the martial art of Remote Viewing.

SCRYING: Using a reflective or semi-reflective surface to "see" paranormal information. (e.g., looking into a crystal ball, or other smooth surfaced reflective pool.) The person actually doesn't see things there, but it provides a good backdrop for the recognition of mental projections or impressions, by otherwise keeping the normal senses occupied.

SENSE: Any use of a normal faculty such as seeing, hearing, smelling, tasting, or touching, as a direct result of internal or external stimuli.

SIGNAL: Information hypothetically being transmitted from the target place, object, person, or event somewhere in space/time.

SIGNAL LINE: Hypothetical line of communication that supposedly carries the information received by the remote viewer. The existence and/or origin of a signal line is actually unknown.

SKEPTICISM: A healthy doctrine that states true knowledge or knowledge in any particular area is always going to be uncertain. A skeptic always retains a certain degree of question or doubt.

SUBCONSCIOUS (Mind): Just outside of consciousness. Part of the mind that possesses information the conscious mind is not aware of or awake to. Hypothetically, the subconscious is that part of the mind which holds the information sought by the conscious mind during remote viewing.

TARGET (SITE): The place, person, object, or event, located somewhere specifically within space/time, which the remote viewer is attempting to provide information on.

Appendix B

———————— ✸ ————————

The following is reprinted with the permission of the Author, S. James P. Spottiswoode, Cognitive Sciences Laboratory, Palo Alto, California. It was originally appeared in *The Journal of Scientific Exploration, Vol II, No. 2, 1997.*

APPARENT ASSOCIATION BETWEEN EFFECT SIZE IN FREE RESPONSE ANOMALOUS COGNITION EXPERIMENTS AND LOCAL SIDEREAL TIME

S. James P. Spottiswoode
Cognitive Sciences Laboratory, Palo Alto, CA 94301

Abstract

Nothing is known about the physical mechanism of anomalous cognition (AC), or ESP. A first step towards generating focused hypotheses would be the discovery of a physical parameter, which clearly modulated AC performance. In this paper, an association between the local sidereal time (LST) at which a trial occurs and the resulting effect size is described. In an existing database of 1,468 free response trials, the effect size increased 340% for trials within 1 hour of 13.5 h LST (p:0,001). An independent database of 1,015 similar trials was subsequently obtained in which trials within 1 hour of 13.5 h LST showed an effect size increase of 450% (p:0.05) providing confirmation of the effect. Possible artifacts due to the non-uniform distribution of trials in clock time and variations of effect size with experiment are discussed and rejected as explanations. Assuming that some unknown systematic bias is not present in the data, it appears that AC performance is strongly dependent upon the LST at which the trial occurs. This is evidence of a causal connection between performance and the orientation of the receiver (i.e., a term for subject or participant), the earth and the fixed stars.

Introduction

Over the last decade of research into anomalous cognition (AC), a new term for extrasensory perception or ESP, considerable progress has been made toward understanding the experimental factors needed to ensure that the effect is observed. In fact the question of existence can now reasonably be said to have been answered positively (Utts, 1996.) In contrast, little headway has been made in understanding the mechanism of the information transfer in physical terms. Currently there are no known physical parameters, which unambiguously modify AC performance, and the discovery of such a variable would be a first step to elucidating the physical mechanisms involved.

From a physics point of view, a puzzling feature of anomalous cognition is that there is not evidence that performance falls off with the distance between receiver and target over separations up to several thousand kilometers (Puthoff and Targ, 1976; Dunne et al., 1989). More problematic still, the evidence for precognitive AC is strong and performance in this situation is comparable to that in real-time protocols; Dunne et al., (1989) show that effect size in their database is independent of the interval between remote viewing session and target definition over a range of ±150 h. Recently, a theory has been developed by May et al. (1995), which explains another class of parapsychological experiments involving attempts to "influence" random systems, in so-called micro-PK experiments. Their model proposes that the results of these experiments are due to a weak precognitive information channel as opposed to a force-like interaction. Thus in looking for some underlying mechanism that might explain all these data, it appears that precognition is a good possibility: the notion encompasses micro-PK effects and precognitive AC results. Data from real time protocols can also be explained by precognition if it is assumed that the signal source is the eventual observation of the correct answer.

Given these properties of the putative physical carrier responsible for anomalous cognition, it is not obvious where one would look amongst known physics for a model or for an extension of fundamental theory that would allow for these effects. It has been suggested that the non-local correlations of quantum mechanics might be used to explain AC (Walker, 1975), but the fact that these correlations do not permit causal signaling rules them out as a mechanism. In searching for a model, knowledge of a physical variable, which modified the performance of the AC channel would be extremely useful.

It is outside the scope of this paper to review the research on physical modulators of AC, but mention will be made of the two most prevalent in the literature. There is weak evidence that performance is enhanced by screening electrical fields with Faraday cages (Tart, 1988) and that it is improved during periods when the geomagnetic field is relatively quiescent (Spottiswoode, 1993). More attention has been paid to the latter effect, but the correlation of AC with the geomagnetic field fluctuations, if it exists at all in laboratory data, is very small. For instance, in the extensive collection of trials examined in this paper the correlation between the *ap* geomagnetic index and AC effect size is small (Spearman's p:-0.05, n:2,483, p:0.01) though in the hypothesized direction. The possibility that performance is affected by a globally averaged parameter like the geomagnetic indices suggest that it might be fruitful to broaden the search for a physical variable describing the environment of the receiver, such as electric or magnetic fields, to the larger scale.

Consider how the data of anomalous cognition might have been approached if, instead of emerging from a protocol based in the psychological sciences, these signals had appeared as sporadic bursts of information from a complex physical experiment. In that case, the effort to find the source of the unexpected signals would have progressed from local sources of noise to an examination of whether the noise were correlated with activity outside the laboratory. A useful technique for achieving this would be to examine whether the sporadic noise were correlated with local time, which might indicate that power fluctuations, ground vibration or other human activity tied to local time were responsible. Failing that, it would be natural to see if the noise were correlated with sidereal time, indicating a cosmic origin. Pulsars were in fact discovered in just this manner. This paper asks this latter question of the AC data and thereby takes a first step in addressing the question of whether performance is dependent upon the receiver's orientation relative to the fixed star background.

The Anomalous Cognition Data

To search for a potential physical correlate of AC functioning requires either large numbers of prospective studies or the retrospective examination of existing data which was collected for other reasons. As collecting high quality anomalous cognition trials is time consuming and expensive, there is a motivation for using existing data where possible. The author had already assembled a database of free response data for another purpose and a subset of these data were suitable for this study; from now on, this will be referred to as the original data set. This original data set comprised results from 22 different studies, which utilized either remote viewing or the ganzfeld protocol and for which exact times, dates and locations of the trails were known. The 1,524 trials in these studies were collected in various laboratories by different experimenters over the last 20 years and are shown in Table 1. Most of these studies have been published in peer reviewed journals, conference proceedings, or laboratory reports. It should be emphasized however, that this collection is not exhaustive of remote viewing and ganzfeld experimentation. The criteria for inclusion in the original data set were merely that the laboratory was able to provide data at the trial level with time, location and score, and that the experiment was of a free response design. The criterion of free response was established in order to collect data with the highest possible effect size and thus maximize the efficiency of the search for a physical correlate. It should be noted that the division into studies was based purely upon the way the experimenter presented the data. In several cases data from a single protocol was presented as a number of experiment series, or studies, while in fact the publication they may have been presented as a single experiment. In some cases the division into series may correspond to a division by receiver, in others to a division by time period.

Table 1. Original Data Set

STUDY	Start Year	End Year	N	Effect Size	Z	P
PEAR	76	84	330	0.33	6.05	7.1×10^{-10}
Schlitz & Gruber	79	79	10	0.56	1.76	0.04
Schlitz & Haight	80	80	10	0.15	0.46	0.3
Carpenter	86	90	90	0.08	0.73	0.2
Edinburgh. Pilot	90	90	69	-0.05	-0.41	0.66
Edinburgh. Training Study	91	91	174	0.07	0.88	0.2
IfP Manual ganzfeld Series 003	86	86	31	-0.28	-1.54	0.9
IfP Manual ganzfeld Series 004	89	89	37	0.12	0.74	0.23
IfP Manual ganzfeld Series 101	86	87	40	0.06	0.36	0.3
IfP Manual ganzfeld Series 987	87	88	48	0.007	0.05	0.5
PRL A	89	89	20	0.68	3.02	0.001
PRL B	87	89	24	0.91	4.45	4.21×10^{-6}
SJPS GMF Study	91	91	101	0.00	0.00	0.5
SJPS PRV	83	83	19	0.66	2.89	0.002
SJPS RAB	84	84	40	0.08	0.51	0.3
SRI Tachistoscope	87	87	160	0.2	2.53	0.006
SRI Precognitive vs Real-Time	87	87	81	-0.07	-0.61	0.7
SRI Hypnosis	87	88	44	-0.07	-0.47	0.6
SRI Fax	87	90	40	0.41	2.57	0.005
Utrecht S1	92	92	50	0.015	0.11	0.4
Utrecht S2	92	93	50	-0.092	-0.65	0.7

Notes:

1. PEAR - Princeton Engineering Anomalies Research, Dept. of Engineering, Princeton University; IfP - Institute for Parapsychology, formerly Foundation for Research on the Nature of Man; PRL - Psychophysical Research Laboratories; SRI - SRI International; SJPS - the author; Utrecht - Parapsychological Institute, Utrecht.

2. Published study Z scores may differ from those shown here due to alternative methods of calculating overall Z.

The contributing laboratories included most of the major centers where free response AC work has occurred. One of the data sets used here, that from the Princeton

Engineering Anomalies Research (PEAR) group, has been subjected to some methodological criticism (Hansen *et al.*, 1992; Bobyns, Y., 1992). However the effect size and associated 95% confidence interval of the PEAR data fall within the range reported by other free-response investigations (Utts, 1996b; Radin, 1996). Therefore, their data were included in the original data set.

This paper examines a relationship between AC performance and the receiver's orientation relative to the celestial sphere and therefore the appropriate celestial coordinate system is briefly reviewed. Directions in the sky are conventionally measured with respect to a coordinate system defined by the earth's rotational axis and equatorial plane. The celestial equator is the projection of the earth's equator onto the sky and the declination of an object is defined as the angle north, or south, of this great circle. An object's right ascension, or RA, is defined as the angle around the celestial equator between the great circle passing through the object and the celestial poles and a fixed point on the celestial equator, the vernal equinox. Thus, declination and RA comprise a coordinate system for the celestial sphere in the same way that latitude and longitude do for the earth's surface. At any given point on the earth's surface the stars return to their same positions after one sidereal day has elapsed, this day being approximately 3' 56" shorter than a solar day.[1] At any location and time, the local sidereal time (LST) is defined as the RA of the meridian that is the great circle, which passes through the zenith and celestial poles. Thus at a same value of LST for any observer, the same strip of sky will be directly overhead.

The trials comprising the AC database occurred at locations in North America and Europe at times and dates

---

[1] The ordinary 24-hour solar day is slightly longer than the sidereal day owing to the revolution of the earth around the Sun in the same direction as the daily rotation of the earth. The earth must rotate a little more to bring the Sun back overhead from one noon to the next since the Sun has advanced slightly with respect to the stars in the course of a day. In the course of a year there is one extra rotation of the earth with respect to the stars compensating for the single yearly revolution around the Sun.

determined by the scheduling of those experiments and entirely unconnected with the purpose of this study. As such they occurred mostly during normal working hours, at various times of the year and therefore covered the whole range of LST values. However, the range of latitudes at which these experiments occurred was quite limited, nearly all the data being taken between 32 and 55 degrees North. Thus the range of declination was similarly restricted. This study therefore sought to examine whether there was any relationship between LST and AC performance.

Method

The received data was first filtered to eliminate cases where the local time was omitted or location information was either absent or very approximate. One entire experiment was removed from the original data set since reliable time information for each trial was not available. This winnowing reduced the data to 1,468 trials from 21 studies for the original data set. SLT values for all trials were calculated from the longitude and given local time of each trial. It should be noted that the time data given by the various experimenters is probably that of the start of each AC trial and may differ from the time of the actual mentation by a few minutes to as much as a quarter of an hour. The majority of trials occurred in laboratories in cities and towns and the longitude for these trials was taken from the values for the city given in an atlas. Local times were corrected for daylight savings time and used to calculate LST by means of the program Xephem version 2.9. As a check, LST values for several randomly chosen points were hand calculated to confirm the accuracy of the software.

The AC score data for the trials was delivered from the various experiments in one of two forms. In some cases an effect size for each trial had been calculated from a quasi-continuous measure used in the experiment. These values were used in this analysis without further processing. In other cases, the trials had been assessed by a ranking procedure in which either the receiver, in the ganzfeld experiments, or an Analyst, in the remote viewing experiments, had rated the receiver's description against the actual target and a number of decoy targets in a blind judging procedure. These trials therefore were scored as a rank, where a value of 1 indicated that the actual target was rated as the closet fit to the receiver's description, 2 as the second closest fit, and so on. These ranks were converted to trial effect sizes by means of the formula:

$$es = \frac{r_{MCE} - r_{OBS}}{\sqrt{(N^2 - 1)/12}}$$

where r_{MCE} is the mean chance expectation rank, r_{OBS} is the observed rank and N is the number of targets used in the ranking procedure. In a few experiments the scores were reported both as quasi-continuous scores obtained from receivers estimating their preference for the target on a scale and as rankings. In these cases the effect sizes calculated by the experimenter from the continuous measure were used rather than computing an effect size from the rank since it is likely that the continuous measure contains more information about the degree of match between description and target than does the rank.

Results—Original Data Set

The original data set had an overall mean effect size of 0.148 (*n*:1,468), corresponding to a Stouffer's Z:5.99, (*p* 7 x 10⁻⁹), while individual study effect sizes ranged from –0.28 up to 0.56. These data were collected into 1-hour wide bins of LST and the mean and standard deviation of the effect size data for each bin were found. An increase in the mean effect size for trials occurring between 13 and 14 h LST was observed. The data are shown boxcar smoothed in Figure 1 where the mean effect size for data points within a 2-hour wide window, moving in 0.1-hour steps, is plotted. When calculating these and subsequent smoothed plots the data set was padded with two copies of itself where the time values were 24 h later and 24 h earlier than the actual time. Thus the averaging occurred over a 2-hour window also for points at the ends of the plots. The dashed line in Figure 1 is the average effect size and the error bars correspond to (1 standard deviation (SD).

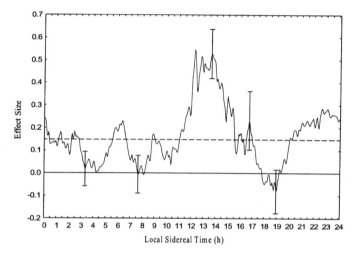

The local sidereal time corresponding to maximum effect size was estimated by computing the centroid of the subset of the data comprising the upper half of the 12 h to 14 h peak and gave a value of 13.47 h. To assess the significance of this deviation from the average effect size of the whole data set, various values of time intervals around 13.47 h were taken and the main effect size of these subsets compared to that of the remainder of the data. The results are show in Table 2 where the gain is calculated as the ratio of the effect size within the chosen time range to the effect size for the complete data set. The *t* values shown compare the data in the subset around the peak with the remainder of the data. For instance, the trials, which occurred within ±1 hour of 13.47 h, showed an average effect size of 0.507 (*n*:83) as compared to the complete data set effect size of 0.148, an increase of effect size by a factor of 3.42.

Table 2. Original Data.

Time period Around 13.47 h	ES	N	Gain	t	df	p (1 - tail)
± 1.0	0.507	83	3.42	2.83	1466	0.001
± 2.0	0.388	131	2.62	2.80	1466	0.005
± 3.0	0.320	194	2.16	2.49	1466	0.01
± 4.0	0.248	283	1.67	1.83	1466	0.07

It appears therefore that the trials occurring within ±3.0 hours, or less, of 13.47 h are significantly different from the remainder of the data and the observed effect size increases the closer the trial time to 13.47 h.

Validation Data: Collection and Results

After the above analysis was completed, it was hypothesized that there was an approximately three to four times enhancement in anomalous cognition effect size for trials occurring near 13.5 h local sidereal time. In order to test this hypothesis against a new set of data, laboratories were contacted with a request for any further free response data meeting the same criteria as used for the original data set. Table 3 shows an additional 23 experiments, which were received comprising 1,015 trials. This data set also shows evidence of AC with an overall effect size of 0.085 (n:1,015), yielding a Stouffer's Z:2.70 (p:0.004).

Table 3. Validation Data Set

STUDY	Start Year	End Year	N	Effect Size	Z	P
SJPS ARV	95	96	216	0.00	-0.01	0.5
Edinburgh - KD	95	96	128	0.48	5.38	3.78×10^{-8}
Edinburgh Sender-No Sender	94	94	97	0.14	1.41	0.08
Amsterdam ganzfeld 1982	82	82	32	0.14	0.79	0.2
Amsterdam ganzfeld 1994	94	94	37	0.31	1.90	0.03
Amsterdam ganzfeld 1995	95	95	68	0.058	0.48	0.3
Amsterdam ganzfeld 1996	96	96	39	-0.22	-1.36	0.9
IfP Manual ganzfeld Series 201	87	87	10	-0.48	-1.51	0.9
IfP Manual ganzfeld Series 202	89	89	20	-0.088	-0.39	0.6
IfP Manual ganzfeld Series 203	90	91	46	0.075	0.51	0.3
IfP Manual ganzfeld Series 301	90	91	20	0.018	0.081	0.5
IfP Manual ganzfeld Series 302	90	91	26	0.15	0.76	0.2
IfP Manual ganzfeld Series 400	87	92	38	-0.018	-0.11	0.5
IfP Manual ganzfeld Series 401	88	88	12	0.38	1.32	0.09
IfP Manual ganzfeld Series 989	89	92	17	0.47	1.96	0.03
IfP Auto ganzfeld Series CLAIR1	94	96	50	-0.064	-0.46	0.7
IfP Auto ganzfeld Series EC1	93	95	51	0.13	0.95	0.2
IfP Auto ganzfeld Series FT1	93	94	50	-0.26	-1.84	0.9
IfP Auto ganzfeld Series FT2	94	95	50	-0.065	-0.46	0.7
IfP Auto ganzfeld Series GEN1	93	94	8	-0.04	-0.11	0.5

Notes:

1. Edinburgh - Koestler Chair of Parapsychology, University of Edinburgh; Amsterdam - Dept. of Psychology, University of Amsterdam.
2. Published study Z scores may differ from those shown here due to alternative methods of calculating overall Z.

These new data were processed through the same analysis as used with the original data set and a smoothed plot of the validation data, using a 2-hour averaging window as before, is shown in Figure 2 along with the original data set for comparison and ±1 SD error bars. The validation data set also has a broad peak in effect size near 13 h and the LST for maximum effect size was found to be 13.47 h, identical to the value found from the original data set. The effect sizes as a function of window width around 13.47 h for the validation data are shown in Table 4.

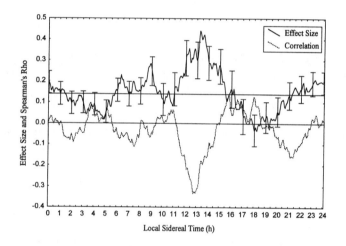

Local Sidereal Time (h)

Table 4. Validation Data

Time period Around 13.47 h	ES	N	Gain	t	df	p (1 - tail)
± 1.0	0.383	43	4.51	1.96	1013	0.05
± 2.0	0.266	83	3.13	1.69	1013	0.09
± 3.0	0.190	136	2.24	1.29	1013	0.20
± 4.0	0.130	191	1.53	0.68	1013	0.50

Results—Combined data sets

Given that the effect sizes and gains shown here for the validation data set are close to those from the original data set and that the LST values corresponding to maximum effect size are not different, it seems reasonable to conclude that the hypothesized peak in effect size has been confirmed in the validation data set. The data sets were therefore combined and the analysis repeated for all the data taken together. In this case the overall effect size is 0.122 (n:2,483) for a Stouffer's Z:6.09 (p:6 x 10^{-10}). Using the same methods as before, the LST for maximum effect size was found to be 13.47 h. The complete data set is plotted with a 2-hour wide averaging window and ±1 SD error bars in Figure 3, with the mean for the whole data set dashed. In a Monte Carlo test the effect sizes were randomly permuted with respect to the time data and the means of all 2-hour wide windows with centers spaced at 0.1-hour intervals were computed. In 10,000 such runs 14 produced a window mean effect size at some value of LST, which was greater than or equal to that seen in the actual data. Thus the probability of finding an effect size peak of the magnitude observed at any value of LST was estimated to be 0.0014. The increase in effect size observed in time windows centered on the maximum is shown in Table 5. As can be seen from these data, it may be possible to increase effect size in AC experiments as much as four-fold by timing them near 13.5 h. The width of the 13.5 h peak was ±1.25 h, measured at half height above the mean. This plot also shows a suggestion of a minimum of effect size occurring near 18 h. It is worth noting that although the data used here are very disparate, both in terms of study effect size and protocol, the subset which were accidentally taken within ±1 h of 13.47 h yield an overall significance of Z:5.20, p:1 x 10^{-7}(n:124).

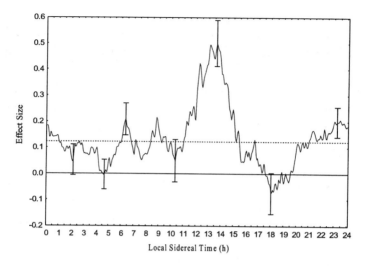

Local Sidereal Time (h)

Table 5. Original and validation data combined.

Time period Around 13.47 h	ES	N	Gain	t	df	p (1 - tail)
± 1.0	0.467	124	3.82	3.85	2481	0.0001
± 2.0	0.353	217	2.88	3.47	2481	0.0005
± 3.0	0.263	331	2.14	2.68	2418	0.007
± 4.0	0.196	472	1.61	1.75	2418	0.08

Replication across studies

To check whether the 13.5 h effect replicated across these studies, the effect size in the region of 13.5 h, and outside this time interval, was calculated for each study. Owing to the small numbers of trials in many of the studies, 15 of the 41 total studies failed to have any data falling in the 13.5 h peak, taken here as 13.47 ±2 h, while one experiment had all its data on the peak and none elsewhere. This study contributed 10 trails with a mean effect size of 0.147. Of the remaining 26 studies, with data both on and off the peak, 18 had a mean effect size on the peak greater than mean effect size for the remainder of the data (p:0.02). There is evidence from other types of parapsychological research that receivers at times significantly miss targets and it is worth noting that 25 out of the 26 studies with data on and off peak had a greater absolute magnitude of effect size on the peak (p:4 x 10^{-7}).

Possible Artifacts

The trials in these studies occurred primarily during office hours, 81% falling between 0900 and 1700 local time. Since the trials occurred throughout the year, the conversion to LST for each trail time effectively smeared the distribution of trial times approximately evenly across the range of LST. One possible explanation for the peak at 13.5 h would be provided if two things were true: that the effect size in this data were dependent on local clock time, and that the trials responsible for the LST peak fell at a value of local time which maximized their effect size.

Figure 4 shows the distribution of effect size as a function of local clock time with the mean of the whole data set dashed. It is apparent that while the effect size in this data is approximately independent of clock time over most of the day, there is an increase in effect size at 6 h; however, this is due to only 4 data points, 3 of which are from one experiment (PEAR) which had a relatively high average effect size of 0.33. In fact the whole region from 3 A.M. to 8 A.M. contains only 18 trials and with such a small number of data points no reliable estimate of the behavior of effect size versus clock time in this period can be made. Four trials from this period fall in the 13.37 ±2 h LST peak and cannot significantly influence the statistics of the 217 trials comprising this region of LST. Apart from this early morning period, the clock-time distribution is statistically flat.

As an alternative way of looking at the impact of the variations in effect size with local time, the data was normalized to remove the variation with clock time. This was achieved by subtracting from each trial's effect size the difference between the overall mean of the data set and the mean for the data in the 1-hour clock time bin containing that point. This normalized data set therefore had a uniform effect size when plotted against clock time in 1-hour bins. When plotted against LST it produced a plot, which was virtually indistinguishable from the un-normalized plot shown in

Figure 3. Thus, any contribution to the LST peak from clock-time variations in effect size is negligible.

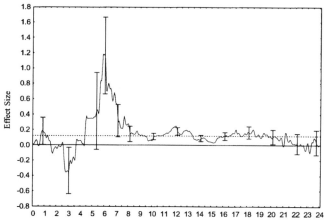

Another possible artifact could be created by an interaction between experiments of differing effect size with restricted ranges of LST values. Due to the slow drifting of LST versus solar time at approximately four minutes a day, an experiment which was scheduled to collect data at the same time every day for, say, a month would produce a data set that all fitted within a two hour slot of LST. If this were an experiment which, for other reasons, produced a high effect size, and where the scheduled times fell near 13 h LST, then the apparent increase of effect size observed at that value of LST would be explained by the arbitrary timing of such a high effect size experiment.

Before addressing this potential artifact, it is worthwhile clarifying some assumptions implicit in this retrospective analysis. It is being assumed that the effect size in an anomalous cognition trial is a function of several parameters: *ES:F(LST,R,E,X)*. Where R is the type of receiver, expert or novice, *E* is the experimenter, *X* represents all other unknown sources of variance and *F* is an unknown but fixed, function. It is also being assumed that in any one experiment R and E were held constant and that R, E and X are not functions of LST. Under the null hypothesis of no LST effect it is presumed that the variation in effect size between studies is due solely to differing values of R, E and X. Utilizing the 26 studies with data on and off the 13.47 ± 2 h peak, the expected value for the average effect size on the peak can then be calculated as the weighted average of individual study effect sizes, where the weighting factor is the number of on-peak trials for each study. This results in a weighted effect size of 0.154, which is not significantly different from the effect size of 0.148 for all the data in the 26 studies. In contrast, the observed effect size on the peak is 0.342 for these 26 studies. Thus, the LST peak cannot be explained by fortuitous combination of R, E and X, or by the happenstance timing of trials in each study. Since LST is a linear function of local solar time and the day of the year, there remains the possibility that some undiscovered systematic relationship between effect size and these variables might be responsible for the observed peak.

Discussion

Evidence has been given to support a relationship between the local sidereal time, at which an anomalous cognition experiment occurs, and the resulting effect size. The primary association is an approximately four-fold enhancement in AC effect size at 13.5 h LST. This association was found in one large data set and confirmed in another, each set comprising AC experiments with a range of free response protocols, from different laboratories and investigators. It is likely that the increase of effect size for AC trials occurring at 13.5 h LST is real, replicable across different laboratories and occurs in the diverse protocols of the ganzfeld and remote viewing experiments.

The discovery of this effect was motivated by the search for a physical parameter, which unambiguously modulated AC performance. What classes of mechanism are suggested by the LST effect found here? The *prima facie* implication is that a causal relationship exists between an unknown influence at a fixed RA in the sky and AC functioning. Such an influence must originate from outside the solar system since within the heliopause the interplanetary space environment is dominated by solar and planetary effects which would not be locked to a fixed RA. Similarly, all known solar system objects have varying positions in the sky; only objects as remote as Neptune and Pluto have moved less than 3 h of RA during the data collection period of this analysis. As to the nature of the influence at fixed RA, there are a wide range of signals potentially available to the appropriate detector at the earth's surface, which are locked to sidereal time. Most of the electromagnetic spectrum from gamma rays through low frequency radio have known cosmic sources. There are also particle fluxes from discrete sources. It may be possible to single out amongst all these emissions a factor at 13.5 h RA, which is associated with the effect described here.

A noteworthy feature of the 13.5 h effect size enhancement is the narrowness of the peak, which was ±1.25 h to half height. As was noted earlier, the trial time data used in this paper may differ from the actual time of the receiver's mentations. Such errors would broaden the peak and the actual effect may therefore be more time sensitive. This argues against the hypothesis that the increase in effect size is due to a region of the sky simply being above the horizon, since if this were the case the peak would be much wider. If the LST effect were dependent on the altitude of a source, then one would expect the width of the peak to be dependent on latitude. Interestingly, when the 13.5 h peak is examined for data taken at high latitudes versus low latitudes there is a suggestion that the peak is narrower for the high latitude data, but this analysis is confounded by the fact that particular laboratories and protocols are being selected by the latitude division. Further work in this direction must await a data set collected with accurate timings of the receiver's mentations, using a consistent protocol and over a wide range of latitudes.

Another implication of this LST effect is that some property of the earth is important to AC functioning. For instance, one class of models that would be consistent with the LST effect would posit an AC-enhancing signal from a direction in space associated with RA:13.5 h and that this signal was at least partially blocked by the earth. An alternative class of models would postulate a signal from a direction opposite to 13.5 h RA acting as an AC inhibitor, though this would result in a broader peak than observed. While it is clearly impossible to reach any conclusions about the mechanism of this effect it would seem that any model must include the earth as a causal part of the mechanism, either as an absorber or reflector. In this regard it is interesting to note that there is evidence that AC performance does not decrease with the distance between target and receiver, at least up to separations of several thousand km and these long-range tests demonstrate that no difference in AC performance is made by interposing the earth between receiver and target.

Assuming that this effect replicates in prospective tests, it will have some important consequences aside form its impact on theory. Parapsychology has struggled to establish its main effect, anomalous cognition, in part because of the small effect size seen in these protocols. The fourfold increase in effect size produced by timing trials at the optimal value of LST will make a considerable difference in designing proof-oriented experiments as well as increasing the statistical power of any experiment looking for other moderating factors.

Much further work needs to be done to elucidate this effect. Prospective tests of the relationship between AC effect size and LST need to be undertaken and in designing these it would be useful to collect data at a range of times around the 13.5 h maximum so that the exact shape of the peak can be found. It may also be important to collect AC data at a wide range of latitudes to see if AC effect size is related to the declination of the zenith at the site of the trials. Evidence of a maximum in effect size versus latitude would suggest that a limited region of the sky, bracketed in both RA and declination, were responsible for modulating anomalous cognition performance.

Acknowledgments
First, I would like to express my deep appreciation to the many laboratories and individual researchers who generously provided their data for this analysis. Some even provided data from work in progress.

The manuscript has seen many iterations and has been significantly improved in content and in form. The contributions of Dr. Edwin C. May—CSL, Professor Jessica Utts—University of California at Davis, Professor Peter Sturrock—Standford University and Dr. Richard Broughton—Institute for Parapsychology are deeply appreciated. This work could not have proceeded without their support and counsel.

References
Dobins, Y. H., Dunne, B. J., Jahn, R. G. and, Nelson, R. D. (1992). Response to Hansen, Utts and Markwick: statistical and methodological problems of the PEAR remote viewing (sic) experiments. *Journal of Parapsychology* 56, 115-146.

Dunne, S. J., Dobyns, Y. H., Intner, S. M. (1989). Precognitive remote perception III: Complete binary data base with analytical refinements. Technical Note PEAR 89002, Princeton University.

Hansen, G. P., Utts, J. and Markwick, B., (1992). Critique of the PEAR remote viewing experiments. *Journal of Parapsychology*, 56, 97-113.

May, E. C., Utts, J. M., Spottiswoode, S. J. P., (1995). Decision augmentation theory: toward a model of anomalous phenomena. *Journal of Parapsychology*, 59, 195-220.

Puthoff, H. E., and Targ, R., (1976). A perceptual channel for information transfer over kilometer distances:

Historical perspective and recent research. *Proceedings of the IEEE*, **64**, 3, 329-354.

Radin, D. I., (1996). A manuscript in preparation for a book. Private communication.

Spottiswoode, S. J. P., (1993). Effect of ambient magnetic field fluctuations on performance in a free-response anomalous cognition task: A pilot study. *Proceedings of the 36th Annual Convention of the Parapsychological Association*, 143-156.

Tart, C. T., (1988). Effects of electrical shielding on GESP performance. *Journal of the American Society for Psychical Research*, **82**, 129-145.

Utts, J. M., (1996a). Science in the age of (mis)information. First World Skeptics Congress, 20th Anniversary of CSICOP, Amherst, New York.

Utts, J. M., (1996b). An evaluation of remote viewing: Research and applications. *Journal of Parapsychology*, **59** (4), 289-320.

Walker, E. H., (1975). Foundations of paraphysical and parapsychological phenomena. In Oteri, L., (Ed.), *Quantum physics and parapsychology* (pp. 1-53). New York: Parapsychology Foundation.

Appendix C

— ✳ —

The following is reprinted with the permission of the Author, S. James P. Spottiswoode, Cognitive Sciences Laboratory, Palo Alto, California. It was originally submitted to *The Journal of Parapsychology*, in 1998.

GEOMAGNETIC FLUCTUATIONS AND FREE RESPONSE ANOMALOUS COGNITION: A NEW UNDERSTANDING

James Spottiswoode
Cognitive Sciences Laboratory, Palo Alto, California

Abstract

Efforts to establish whether a correlation between anomalous cognition (AC) performance and geomagnetic fluctuations (GMF) exists have met with mixed results, a negative correlation being seen in some studies and not in other comparable ones. Confirming this observation, in a large database of 2,879 free-response trials the Spearman's ρ correlation between the *ap* geomagnetic index and AC effect size was -0.029 (p:0.06). However, a large increase in the magnitude of the correlation was found at approximately 13 hours Local Sidereal Time (LST), the longitudinal-like astronomical coordinate for the portion of the celestial sphere that is directly overhead at the time of the viewing. This sharp increase of correlation may be connected with an earlier result: that the AC-effect size increases by 380% within ±1 hour of 13.5 LST. The correlation observed here for trials which occurred between 11.2 h and 14.8 h LST was −0.192 (N:256, p:0.002) while the correlation was effectively zero (ρ:-0.01, N:2,623, ns) elsewhere. The maximum magnitude correlation of -0.33 (N:134, p:0.0001) was observed in the 12.9 (1 h LST period. The negative correlation peak was confirmed in both the ganzfeld and remote viewing protocols and was homogeneously present in those individual studies with trials in the relevant sidereal time interval. This finding allows an understanding of a previous anomaly in the literature: the varying correlations to GMF found in different studies. For instance one large remote viewing study showed near zero overall correlation since few of the trials occurred in the critical time period. In another case a comparable study had a large correlation of -0.22 and by happenstance all the trials were conducted near 13 h LST.

Introduction

For some years there has been speculation that anomalous cognition (AC) performance may be correlated with global geomagnetic field (GMF) fluctuations. This idea arose from the work of Persinger (e.g. 1988) who found that anecdotal cases of putative AC occurred on days when GMF fluctuations were significantly lower than on the preceding and following days. Many workers have investigated whether this interesting observation could be extended to laboratory anomalous cognition, but with mixed results. Tart (1988) and Persinger & Krippner (1989) found an association between high scoring AC trials and low GMF fluctuations, while Haraldsson and Gissurarson (1987) and Nelson & Dunne (1986) did not. In an unpublished meta-analysis this author collected 1,468 free response trials from 21 studies reasoning that the effect, if it existed, would be most easily detected in a large database with high effect size; in fact the overall correlation was a disappointing -0.0002 (Spearman's ρ, N:1,468, ns).

The first step to understanding the physics of anomalous cognition will probably be the discovery of physical variables that unambiguously modulate the effect. In searching for a new approach to the problem of finding such physical variables the author was led to consider whether the orientation in space of the subject might be a factor. Recently it has been shown that there is a relationship between free-response effect size and the Local Sidereal Time (LST) at which a trial occurs (Spottiswoode, 1997). In a database of 2,483 free response trials with a mean effect size of 0.122 overall, those trials that occurred within ±1h of 13.5 h LST showed a 380% increase in effect size. In light of this, it was considered worthwhile revisiting the correlation between anomalous cognition performance and geomagnetic fluctuations but including LST as a filtering variable.

Method
Data Sets

The data consisted of 51 free-response studies comprising 2,879 trials, with a mean effect size of 0.140 and resulting Stouffer's Z of 7.503 (p:3.1 x 10^{-14}). These records were elicited in response to a request for formal experiments (i.e. excluding exploratory trials) that were of free-response design and for which trial time, date, location and score were available. The data falls into two broad groups of protocols. The first includes most of the ganzfeld work done since the 1980s, comprising the complete data from The Psychophysical Research Laboratories, and partial data from The Institute for Parapsychology, the Amsterdam Psychology Department, the Utrecht Institute for Parapsychology and the Koessler Chair at Edinburgh University. The other major grouping consists of remote viewing trials and consists of the work of the Princeton Engineering Anomalies Research, a partial set of data from SRI International and Science Applications International Corporation, experiments by M. S. Schlitz and remote viewing experiments by the author. An exception to this division by protocol is

Carpenter's work, which was obtained in a psychothera-peutic setting. The PEAR remote viewing experiments have been subjected to some methodological criticism (Hansen *et al*, 1992; Dobyns, Y., 1992) but they are included here since the effect size observed is comparable to that seen in other laboratories using a similar protocol.

This data set is not exhaustive of free response experi-mentation, though it likely comprises more than 80% of all such work done in the U.S. and Europe during the last two decades. Rather the data collection effort is part of an ongoing research effort to elucidate physical factors in AC and it is expected that more trials will be added as they are excavated from archives.

Analysis Technique

Each trial's time was corrected for daylight savings time, where appropriate, and converted to Universal Time Coordinated (UTC). Geographical coordinates for the trials were obtained from the gazetteer of the *Rand McNally International Atlas* and this data, with the UTC timings, were used to compute the local sidereal time of each trial. Geomagnetic index data for the *ap* index was obtained from the National Geophysical Data Center as the "Lenhart" data files. The anomalous cognition data was delivered with a time for each trial and a score, given either as ranking made from within a number of choices, or as a trial z-score or effect size. In those cases where a trial effect size was given it was used directly, but when only a ranking was available, it was converted by the stan-dard formula to an effect size:

$$es = \frac{r_{MCE} - r_{OBS}}{\sqrt{(N^2 - 1)/12}}$$

where r_{MCE} is the mean chance expectation rank, r_{OBS} is the observed rank and N is the number of targets used in the ranking procedure.

In the case of many of the ganzfeld trials, such as those using the auto-ganzfeld protocol, the mentation period commenced after a relaxation, or induction tape lasting 15 minutes had been played. In those experiments where this was known to be the case, the stated trial time was adjusted forward by 0.25 h.

The *ap<* index is reported for 3 hour intervals of universal time and the correlation coefficients reported here were calculated between the *ap* index for the 3 hour interval encompassing the trial and AC effect size. In all cases the rank order based, Spearman's ρ correlation function was used, rather than Pearson's *r* to allow for the statistical properties of the *ap* index (Spottiswoode, 1993).

Results

The distribution of correlation in LST space was examined by calculating the correlation between effect size and *ap* in 2 hour wide windows of LST. This calculation was repeated for windows spaced 0.1 h apart for all values of LST from 0h to 24 h. To ensure that windows with their centers in the 0 to 1 h and 23 to 24 h time intervals had a complete set of trials, the LST data was padded with two copies of itself, with the sidereal times advanced and retarded by 24 hours. Figure 1 shows the resulting correlation data plotted against the window center time. The overall correlation of the data (ρ:-0.029, N:2,879, *p*:0.06, 1-tailed) is shown dashed. The error bars show the estimated standard deviation of the correlation coefficients (Hedges & Olkin, 1985) calculated as:

$$\sigma = \sqrt{(1-\rho^2)^2/n}$$

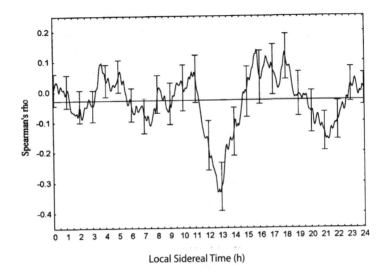

Local Sidereal Time (h)

Correlation between *ap* and effect size versus LST.

The correlation between AC and *ap* geomagnetic index turns out to be strongly dependent on the region of sidereal time considered and there exists substantial correlation near the 13 h point where the maximum effect size was found. The maximum magnitude correlation of -0.33 (N:134, p:0.0001) occurs at 12.9 h, in approximate agreement with the maximum of effect size for this data at 13.3 h. Elsewhere in LST space there is little correlation. Taking as the correlation region the period between 11.2 h and 14.8 h LST, where the correlation shown in Figure 1 crosses zero, the correlation in this "in-band" was -0.192, N:256, p:0.002, whereas the correlation outside was -0.010 (N:2,623, ns). It is interesting to see how this pattern replicates across the individual studies in the database. Table 1 shows the correlations observed in those studies that had five or more trials occurring within this in-band, in order of increasing standard deviation of the estimated in-band correlation.

Table 1 — Correlations by Study

Study	Overall ρ	In-band ρ	σ	N	Out-band ρ	σ	N
Princeton (PEAR)	0.0025	-0.27	0.13	52	0.075	0.06	280
Amsterdam auto-ganzfeld1994	0.045	-0.82	0.14	5	0.14	0.17	32
IfP auto-ganzfeld Series FT2	-0.40	-0.60	0.21	9	-0.38	0.13	41
Utrecht ganzfeld (PA1993)	-0.15	-0.27	0.24	15	-0.11	0.17	35
PRL ganzfeld Series 301	0.14	0.43	0.25	11	0.086	0.16	39
PRL ganzfeld Series 103	0.013	-0.51	0.26	8	0.12	0.15	42
IfP auto-ganzfeld Series CLAIR1	-0.12	-0.40	0.28	9	-0.0012	0.16	41
SJPS ARV	-0.14	-0.10	0.29	12	-0.14	0.069	200
Schlitz & Gruber	-0.22	-0.22	0.30	10	–	–	0
IfP manual ganzfeld Series 203	-0.0081	0.025	0.30	11	-0.015	0.17	35
SRI Precognition vs real-time	0.15	0.084	0.30	11	0.12	0.12	70
SRI Fax study	-0.16	-0.13	0.30	11	-0.046	0.19	29
SAIC Entropy II	0.051	0.40	0.32	7	0.028	0.11	83
Edinburgh auto-ganzfeld	0.14	0.24	0.33	8	0.14	0.089	120
PRL ganzfeld Series 101	0.053	-0.43	0.33	6	0.086	0.15	44
IfP manual ganzfeld Series 301	-0.29	-0.34	0.33	7	-0.30	0.25	13
Carpenter	0.092	-0.042	0.35	8	0.094	0.11	82
PRL ganzfeld Series 104	0.18	0.37	0.35	6	0.18	0.15	41
IfP manual ganzfeld Series 988	0.34	0.21	0.36	7	0.28	0.19	23
IfP manual ganzfeld Series 987	-0.012	0.12	0.37	7	-0.068	0.16	41
SRI Hypnosis study	0.16	-0.23	0.42	5	0.23	0.15	39

The in-band negative correlation is present in many cases where the overall study correlation is near zero or positive. For instance in the large study from PEAR, with an AC effect size of 0.33, the GMF correlation is close to zero for the whole study but clearly seen in the in-band. In a different situation were Schlitz & Gruber, whose data were fortuitously taken entirely in the in-band giving a large correlation to ap, and a large study effect size. The 21 estimates of in-band correlation from these studies were converted to Z scores by means of Fisher's transformation in order to test for homogeneity. The resulting χ^2 (2.66, 20 df, ns) suggests that the same correlation effect was present in these studies, but this result must be treated cautiously as the sample sizes in the critical region of LST are very small for many of these studies. Comparing the protocols in this sample, for ganzfeld data the overall correlation across all trials was -0.023, (N:1609, ns), whereas in the in-band (:-0.18, (N:145, p:0.03). In the case of remote viewing, the correlation of all the data was -0.032 (N:1,254, ns) while the in-band correlation was -0.21 (N:113, p:0.03). The correlation effect at 12.9 h therefore also replicates across these protocols. Finally, it is worthwhile examining the subset of the data that occurred with ±1 h of 12.9 h. These occurred during a wide range of geomagnetic conditions with *ap* values ranging from 0 to 56 and the trials which occurred at times of low <*ap* constitute a highly significant subset. See Table 2 for details. Particularly considering the heterogeneous data analyzed here, these results suggest that unusually high effect sizes may be observed in trials occurring in this time period when geagnetic fluctuations are also minimal.

Table 2 — Effect Size for the Period 11.9 to 13.9 h LST.

ap range	Mean effect size	Stouffer's Z	n	p
0–5	0.71	4.93	48	4.1×10^{-7}
0–10	0.52	4.75	83	1.0×10^{-6}
0–20	0.47	4.92	111	4.4×10^{-7}
0–40	0.36	4.04	128	2.5×10^{-5}

Discussion

The negative correlation between AC effect size and geomagnetic index has been found to be restricted to a limited region of local sidereal times and is effectively absent from this data outside this range. Given that the correlation is observed over approximately 4 h of LST, or 17% of all possible trial times, it is hardly surprising that retrospective searches for the effect in experiments timed without regard for this result have yielded conflicting results.

Figure 2 shows the distribution of AC effect size versus local sidereal time with the correlation to *ap* superimposed. The mean effect size in the AC data of 0.140 is shown dashed.

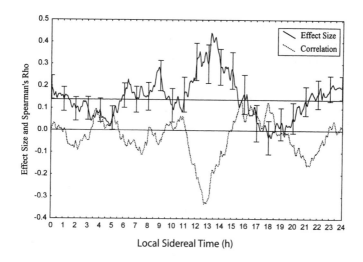

Effect Size and Correlation to *ap* versus LST.

As can be seen the maximum in effect size occurs a little later (es:0.434 at 13.3 h) than the maximal correlation (ρ :-0.334 at 12.9 h), though this cannot be established definitely given the noise in the data. It should be noted that the apparently very strong inverse relationship between effect size and correlation seen in Figure 2 is partly an artifact, since the effect size data contributes to both the correlation and mean effect plots. What seems to be occurring is that as the anomalous cognition improves near 13 h, the signal comes up out of the noise and the correlation strengthens.

It should be noted that the occurrence of this correlation between *ap* and effect size in a restricted region of LST does not imply that the trials responsible for the correlation peak occurred at similar local times. The 2,879 trials studied here occurred at all times of the day and year over two decades and the transformation from local to sidereal time has taken any particular value of local time into all regions of LST. Conversely, the trials responsible for the 13 h correlation and effect size peaks occurred at all times of the day. Therefore physiological and other factors, which are correlated with the local time for each subject, cannot be responsible for the 13 h peak.

The existence of this correlation is puzzling. The global geomagnetic indices, such as *ap*, measure fluctuations occurring over time periods of a few minutes to some hours in the strength of the earth's magnetic field averaged around the globe. At any particular location, typical disturbances produce changes in field strength of the order of 50—200 nT in a total field strength of approximately 50,000 nT. The subjects in these experiments were typically in urban environments where field changes due to buildings and ferrous structures can be many times larger than this and occur rapidly as the body moves through steep field gradients. It thus seems improbable that the geomagnetic fluctuations are themselves responsible for the modulation of AC performance. The surface level field fluctuations are one result of complex interactions between emissions of particles and radiation from the sun and earth's field. It is likely that the correlation with anomalous cognition reported here is due to some other parameter associated with these interactions.

The discovery of this effect was motivated by the search for physical variables, which unambiguously modulated AC performance. We are now in possession of two: AC effect size is strongly dependent upon the LST of the receiver and in the limited region of LST where effect is enhanced, the effect size is likely modulated by solar activity, as reflected in the GMF index. While it is premature to speculate as to the mechanism responsible for these effects, but it is clear that the underlying machinery must include a causative agent whose right ascension (the longitude-like coordinate on the celestial sphere) has remained approximately constant through the 20 years of data analyzed here.

Acknowledgments

The greatest thanks are due to all those colleagues who carefully collected and checked the data used here and kindly made it available for this study.

References

Dobyns, Y. H., Dunne, B. J., Jahn, R. G. and Nelson, R. D., (1992). Response to Hansen, Utts and Markwick: statistical and methodological problems of the PEAR remote viewing (sic) experiments. *Journal of Parapsychology*, 56, 115-146.

Downey, E. C., (1997). Xephem V3.0 at http//iraf.noao.edu/~ecdowney/xephem.html. Dunne, S. J., Dobyns, Y. H., Intner, S. M. (1989). Precognitive remote perception III: Complete binary data base with analytical refinements. Technical Note PEAR 89002, Princeton University.

Hansen, G. P., Utts, J. and Markwick, B., (1992). Critique of the PEAR remote viewing experiments. *Journal of Parapsychology*, 56, 97-113.

Haraldsson E. and Gissurarson, L. R., (1987). Does geomagnetic activity affect extrasensory perception? *Journal of Personality and Individual Differences*, 8, 745-747.

Hedges, L. V. and Olkin, I., (1985). Statistical methods for meta-analysis. Orlando: Academic Press.

Nelson, R. D. and Dunne, B. J., (1986). Attempted correlation of engineering anomalies with global geomagnetic activity. *Proceedings of the 29th Annual Convention of the Parapsychological Association*, 509-518.

Persinger, M. A. and Schaut, G. B., (1988). Geomagnetic factors in subjective telepathic, precognitive, and postmortem experiences. *Journal of the American Society for Psychical Research*, 82, 217-235.

Persinger, M.A. and Krippner, S., (1989) Dream ESP experiments and geomagnetic activity. *Journal of the American Society for Psychical Research*, 83, 101-116.

Spottiswoode, S. J. P., (1993). Effect of ambient magnetic field fluctuations on performance in a free response anomalous cognition task: A pilot study. *Proceedings of the 36th Annual Convention of the Parapsychological Association,* 143-156.

Spottiswoode, S. J. P., (1997). Association between effect size in free response anomalous cognition and local sidereal time. *The Journal of Scientific Exploration* (in press).

Tart, C. T., (1988). Geomagnetic effects on GESP: Two studies. *Journal of the American Society for Psychical Research,* **82,** 193-215.

Appendix D

***

Timing and Protocol Sheets for Remote Viewing

The following are outlines for protocols to be used in remote viewing. They are examples of timing, and actions to be taken by different individuals during the remote viewing process. Where there are differences between training and applications, they are noted.

Outbounder Remote Viewing

Requires:

TARGET POOL: This is a collection of local sites with directions on how to get to them. They are individually sealed within envelopes and are randomly chosen by the Outbounder just prior to going to the actual target site. Formally or informally, the envelope should not be opened until ten to fifteen minutes after the outbounder leaves the lab or location in which the remote viewing is going to take place. In a formal experiment, the person who creates the target pool usually does not participate beyond that. Target pools usually contain at least a few dozen target locations at any given time. Locations can be re-used but only when there is a sufficient number of them to prevent analytic overlay problems for the viewer.

OUTBOUNDER: An individual who travels to the target site. S/he never communicates where they are going with anyone else participating in the remote viewing, until after the remote viewing has been completed.

REMOTE VIEWER: Person who actually does the remote viewing. Is always totally blind to where the target site might be, until after the remote viewing has been completed.

MONITOR: Person who sits in the room with the remote viewer while the remote viewing session is going on. This person is always totally blind to where the target site might be, until after the remote viewing has been completed. (A monitor is only required in research.)

ANALYST: Person who evaluates whether information was passed during a remote viewing. This person is always blind to the target site until after they have performed their analysis. (The Analyst is only required in research.)

Other rules:

Time: Always begins and ends at a specified time.

Participants: Outbounder, Remote Viewer, and Monitor are allowed to visit the actual site once the remote viewing has been completed for feedback and learning purposes. The Analyst may visit the site, but only when visiting a number of sites in order to make a best match evaluation to the remote viewer's materials. The Analyst of course is not told which site was the actual target prior to completion of their analysis.

Evaluation: These targets are formally evaluated when they are done for research purposes. The viewers informally evaluate such targets during their feedback visit during training. They are almost never used for applications purposes.

Example of a time line:

08:20 A.M.   Viewer arrives at lab (or place of viewing).

08:25 A.M.   Viewer and Monitor are secured in room.

08:30 A.M.   Outbounder departs lab.

08:55 A.M.   Outbounder arrives at random target location.

09:00 A.M.   Viewer begins remote viewing, as Outbounder interacts with target location.

09:30 A.M.   Viewer terminates remote viewing, as Outbounder leaves target location.

(Note: The amount of time for remote viewing isn't regulated. The outbounder generally leaves the target site after 30 minutes, but will have no contact with the viewer or monitor until the remote viewing session has been terminated.)

09:35 A.M.   Remote viewing materials are formally logged in, or sealed.

10:00 A.M.   Outbounder returns to the lab (or remote viewing location).

10:05 A.M.   Outbounder, Remote Viewer, and Monitor return to the targeted site for feedback.

(Note: If it is a formal experiment, the viewer is allowed to carry copies of his original viewing notes and drawings— the originals are always retained by the lab. If it is informal, the remote viewer just carries along his notebook. If formal analysis is required, it is carried out by someone who is not present for the remote viewing, and they do not communicate with any of the other participants relevant to the target site, or results, prior to their analysis.)

Non-Outbounder Remote Viewing

Requires:

TARGET POOL: This is a collection of local or distant sites that can be visited physically or through the use of photographs. The locations are individually sealed within envelopes and are randomly chosen by an experimenter just prior to remote viewing taking place. Formally or informally, the envelope is never opened until after the remote viewing has been completed. In a formal experiment, the person who creates the target pool usually does not participate beyond that. Target pools usually contain at least a few dozen-target locations at any given time. Locations can be re-used but only when there is a sufficient number of them to prevent analytic overlay problems for the viewer.

EXPERIMENTER: Person who actually insures a protocol is followed. They will usually select the specific target envelope, but they do not participate in any other part of the effort.

REMOTE VIEWER: Person who actually does the remote viewing. Is always totally blind to where the target site might be, until after the remote viewing has been completed.

MONITOR: Person who sits in the room with the remote viewer while the remote viewing session is going on. This person is always totally blind to where the target site might be, until after the remote viewing has been completed. (A monitor is only required in research.)

ANALYST: Person who evaluates whether information was passed during a remote viewing. This person is always blind to the target site until after they have performed their analysis. (The Analyst is only required in research and formal applications.)

Other rules:

Time: Always begins and ends at a specified time.

Participants: Remote Viewer and Monitor are allowed to visit the actual site, or see the photographs of the site, once the remote viewing has been completed, for feedback and learning purposes. The Analyst may visit the site or see the photographs, but only when visiting a number of sites, or looking at numerous site photographs in order to make a best match evaluation to the remote viewer's materials. The Analyst of course is not told which site was the actual target prior to completion of their analysis.

Evaluation: These targets are formally evaluated when they are done for research purposes. The viewers informally evaluate such targets during their feedback visit, or while looking at the representative photographs during training. In applications, feedback is never provided until after it becomes known that the remote viewer will have no reason for revisiting the site at a later date or time.

Example of a time line:

08:20 A.M.   Viewer arrives at lab (or place of viewing).

08:25 A.M.   Experimenter selects a target envelope.

(Note: S/he can provide or not provide the envelope to the viewer and monitor. As long as it is well-sealed it really doesn't matter.)

08:30 A.M.   Viewer and Monitor are secured in room.

08:40 A.M.   Viewer begins remote viewing.

09:10 A.M.   Viewer terminates remote viewing.

(Note: Aside from a specified start time, the amount of time allowed for the remote viewing isn't regulated.)

09:15 A.M.   Remote viewing materials are formally
              logged in, or sealed.

09:20 A.M.   Remote Viewer and Monitor are allowed to
              open the envelope and then either visit the
              site, or look at the photographs.

(Note: If it is a formal experiment, the viewer is allowed to have copies of his original viewing notes and drawings—the originals are always retained by the lab. If it is informal, the remote viewer just uses the originals or his notes for comparison. If formal analysis is required, it is carried out by someone who is not present for the remote viewing, and they do not communicate with any of the other participants relevant to the target site, or results, prior to their analysis.)

Applications Protocol

Requires:

TARGETING MATERIAL: This is material that is provided by the customer. It insures a direct link to the actual target for the viewer and it can be anything. In a lab, the Experimenter is the only person with direct access to the targeting materials. In applications, it is the person responsible for tasking the viewer, the Tasker. They use these materials to create a target for the remote viewer. The viewer and monitor are always blind to the targeting materials.

EXPERIMENTER/TASKER: Person who actually insures a protocol is followed. They create the target envelope or assign the coordinates that relate to the specific materials used for targeting the viewer. They do not participate in the remote viewing.

REMOTE VIEWER: Person who actually does the remote viewing. Is always totally blind to what the target might be, until after the remote viewing has been completed.

MONITOR: Person who sits in the room with the remote viewer while the remote viewing session is going on. This person is also blind to what the target might be, until after the remote viewing has been completed. (A monitor is not required for applications, but can be used.)

ANALYST: Person who evaluates whether information was passed during a remote viewing. This person is always blind to the target site until after they have performed their analysis. (The Analyst is only required in research and formal applications.)

Other rules:

Time: Always begins and ends at a specified time.

Participants: Remote Viewer and Monitor are provided with the targeting materials once the remote viewing problem has been solved, for feedback and learning purposes. The Analyst will have access to the targeting materials while evaluating the remote viewing materials.

Evaluation: These targets are formally evaluated each time a remote viewing is accomplished. The viewers informally evaluate such targets during their feedback process, but feedback is never provided until after it becomes known that the remote viewer will have no reason for revisiting the site at a later date or time.

Example of a time line:

08:20 A.M.   Viewer arrives at lab (or place of viewing).

08:25 A.M.   Experimenter/tasker provides the target coordinates or envelope.

(Note: S/he can provide or not provide the envelope to the viewer and monitor. As long as it is well sealed it really doesn't matter.)

08:30 A.M.   Viewer and Monitor are secured in room.

08:40 A.M.   Viewer begins remote viewing.

09:10 A.M.   Viewer terminates remote viewing.

(Note: Aside from a specified start time, the amount of time allowed for the remote viewing isn't regulated.)

09:15 A.M.   Remote viewing materials are formally logged in, then passed to the Anlayst.

09:20 A.M.   Remote Viewer and Monitor are allowed to review the targeting materials, as long as there is no further viewing required.

(Note: Feedback to the viewer can be information about what's correct about the viewing information, or how the viewing information proved to be of value. Feedback is only provided after no other requirement for further viewing exists.)

Photographs as Targets

There are some additional comments that are pertinent with regard to photographs being used as targets. *Photographic targets* are not the same as Photographs *of* targets.

Having lots of photographs of a target is not the same as visiting it for feedback. Because there is a substantial loss of quality in the data depending on which kind of targeting is being done, it can have a substantial effect on training.

When training, it is better to use:

First—Outbounder targets.

Second—Photographs of a target location.

Third—Photographs as the target.

When using photographs either to identify the specific target location, or as the actual target, the non-outbounder or applications protocol is applicable.

Coordinate Targets

Coordinate targets are where information written on the sealed envelope is used to identify the specific target of interest. It can be alpha or numeric, or a combination of both. This identifying data has no relationship to what is contained within the envelope. The envelope may contain a photograph of a person, a place, the physical address for a location, a printed question, someone's social security number, a lock of hair, almost anything that will direct the remote viewer to the target of interest.

The protocol for coordinate targets can be the same as that used for the non-outbounder or applications type of targeting.

Associative Remote Viewing Protocol

This is a form of remote viewing that is used to answer binary questions, like; "Yes or No", "Buy or Sell", "Stop or Go."

Requires:

TARGETING MATERIAL: This is material that is provided by the customer. It is usually a binary question, something that requires a choice between two issues. In a lab, the Experimenter is the only person with direct access to a forced choice question. In applications, it is the person responsible for tasking the viewer, the Tasker. The viewer and monitor are always blind to the question being asked as well as the targets selected by the experimenter or Tasker.

EXPERIMENTER/TASKER: Person who actually insures a protocol is followed. They decide based on the original question being asked, which specific targets will represent which specific result pertinent to the question.

As an example, the question being asked is, "Do I invest in Mickey Management, or don't I?"

YES = Assigns a fire truck as the target.

NO = Assigns a basketball auditorium as the target.

They then decide what specific action will determine which target it *should have been* at some point in future time. As an example, next July 1st they will review the stockmarket report for Mickey Management to see if it was profitable enough to be invested in. So, the targeting statement provided directly to the viewer is as follows:

"On July 1st next year, I will take you somewhere and show you something. Describe that something to me."

They do not participate in the remote viewing.

REMOTE VIEWER: Person who actually does the remote viewing. Is always totally blind to what the target might be, until July 1st next year.

MONITOR: Person who sits in the room with the remote viewer while the remote viewing session is going on. This person is also blind to what the target might be. (A Monitor is not required for ARV applications, but can be used.)

ANALYST: Person who evaluates whether information was passed during a remote viewing. They are given the remote viewers perceptions as well as information on the two target possibilities. They are not privy to the reason for the two targets existence. They determine which of the two targets the viewer's material best describes. They provide this information to the Experimenter/Tasker who then reports the answer back to the customer.

Other rules:

Time: Always begins and ends at a specified time. Always has an eventual date when ground truth will be known about what should have been the appropriate response. (In this case July 1st next year—through review of the stock market reports on Mickey Management.)

Participants: Remote Viewer and Monitor are provided with a visit to the actual target on July 1st, which is decided based on what the stock market says should have been done. If the stock did very well, it is a yes, and the viewer is taken to a fire station to see a fire truck. If it did poorly, the viewer is taken to a basketball stadium for feedback.

Evaluation: These targets are formally evaluated each time a remote viewing is accomplished. The viewers informally evaluate such targets during their feedback process only. Feedback in this case will not come until July the 1st, one year later. ARV targets can be set up for learning purposes, in which case the protocol operates exactly the same as for an application.

Example of a time line:

July 1, 2000   Specific date when stock market will dictate if Mickey Management should have been invested in.

July 1, 1999   Actual ARV remote viewing date.

08:00 A.M.   Experimenter/Tasker decides what two targets will be (fire truck for yes, basketball stadium for no).

08:30 A.M.   Viewer arrives at lab (or place of viewing).

08:35 A.M.   Experimenter/Tasker provides the target statement to viewer and monitor, in an envelope."Describe what I will take you to and show you at 09:15 a.m. on July 1, 2000."

(Note: No sealed envelope is really necessary, the viewer just needs to be provided the statement in some way at time of remote viewing.)

08:40 A.M.   Viewer and Monitor are secured in room.

(Note: Monitor can tell viewer the tasking. Or, in the absence of a Monitor, the Viewer simply opens the paper or envelope and reads the tasking.)

08:50 A.M.   Viewer begins remote viewing.

09:10 A.M.   Viewer terminates remote viewing.

(Note: Aside from a specified start time, the amount of time allowed for the remote viewing isn't regulated.)

09:15 A.M.   Remote viewing materials are formally logged in, then passed to the Analyst.

09:20 A.M.   Experimenter/Tasker passes two possible targets to Analyst.

09:30 A.M.   Analyst reports which target was described by viewer to the Experimenter/Tasker.

09:45 A.M.   Experimenter/Tasker reports to customer Yes or No, dependent upon the target described.

(Note: The process is terminated here, and does not continue until July 1, 2000.)

July 1, 2000   (Feedback portion of viewing from one year earlier.)

09:00 a.m.   Remote viewer (and Monitor if desired) report to lab.

09:05 a.m.   Experimenter/Tasker checks stock market reports for Mickey Management.

09:10 a.m.   Experimenter/Tasker, Remote Viewer (and Monitor if desired) drive to fire station.

09:15 a.m.   Viewer is shown fire truck and told if s/he was right or wrong.

(Note: The viewer is never told what the other target was, regardless of whether they were right or wrong. The viewer is always shown the target that it should have been based on outcome. Feedback should always take place at the prescribed time and on the right date.)

Remote Viewing Using Dowsing

When dowsing is used for remote viewing, it can be done either before the remote viewing is done, or after. If it is done prior to the remote viewing, then the dowsing is always done blind—but immediately after being handed the sealed envelope, or told the targeting coordinates.

If the dowsing is scheduled to follow the remote viewing, then it should be done prior to any feedback being given to anyone participating in the remote viewing. All dowsing is done while following the remote viewing protocol for applications.

Training in dowsing should always be done blind, and follow the same rules and structure that is used for the applications protocol.

Maps used for dowsing can front-load a viewer with information pertinent to the actual target they will soon be remote viewing, therefore it is always better to do the dowsing after the remote viewing has been accomplished. By then, the Remote Viewer will have developed a much stronger psychic sense about the target and what it might be, which only improves the results of the dowsing.

The viewer should be as blind as possible to the target while dowsing. Almost any information provided up front will overlay the process with logic, and defeat the entire purpose for dowsing.

Controlled Remote Veiwing (CRV)

The appropriate protocol for use with Controlled Remote Viewing is the applications protocol. While there is a specific interaction that takes place between the Remote Viewer and the monitor, neither should be privy to specifics about the target.

Having said this, I now have to say that the training in CRV is totally different. While being trained in CRV, the trainer (or monitor) knows what the actual target is. The system was designed in such a way as to incorporate a specific set of responses between the Remote Viewer and the trainer. This was done in order to be able to *entrain* the viewer with certain unconscious or autonomic responses.

There are arguments that are positive and negative with regard to such a practice. Those in favor say this form of training helps to entrain the subconscious mind to respond with appropriate information without having the information spoiled with cognitive processing—e.g., injecting fantasy or overlay into the process. Those against, say that the process itself is fantasy, in that all one learns is how to respond to the person sitting across from them neurolinguistically. In other words, the information is passed nonverbally from the person who knows what the target is to the person who doesn't, without the need for psychic functioning.

Rather than enter this debate, I will state emphatically that in order to operate psychically, one must operate within a protocol that necessitates being psychic. So, regardless how you might be trained, when you are *applying remote viewing*, the target should be blind to whomever is in the room.

In my humble opinion, there are no perfect training scenarios when it comes learning remote viewing. They all have their failings and good points. But, when it comes to applications, the only protocols that are valid are the ones that are scientifically proven.

The appropriate protocol for use with CRV is the applications protocol outlined above.

Appendix E

Remote Influencing, Manifestations, and Apparitions

Lots of interesting things that happen around remote viewing are almost never talked about, or are talked about in hushed and worried tones, implying that something is going on that shouldn't be, or that some kind of danger is involved. I'm not sure why people have to bring so much mystery, paranoia, and fear into the subject, but they do. Most of it centers about remote influencing (which includes healing, or by default, wounding), invasive or manipulative entities or manifestations, and directly affecting the future for yourself or others.

Because of the very nature of these subjects, many have their own opinions regarding them. One has only to look at the Internet to see this is so. What I will say about them is based purely on my own observations from twenty-one years of involvement, both in the obtaining of information and in research.

Remote Influencing

Let me start by stating that in only a handful of cases do I believe I've seen remote influencing demonstrated.

Having said this, I can add that in some of those cases, not all the arguments are in, not all of the leakage paths have been sealed, and no one is really sure that remote influencing has actually been displayed. Why?

Well, primarily, as Dean Radin, Ph.D., states in his book *The Conscious Universe* (Harper Collins, 1997, p.132), "no one has been able to design an experiment that will cleanly separate 'pure' precognition from 'pure' mind-matter interaction."

This means there are two things that can always be happening. A subject can be using precognition to *predict* when a variance from the norm will occur, or can be *causing* the variance by direct mental intervention. A formal experiment to differentiate between the two has not yet been designed, at least not one that I'm aware of.

As an example of how this might work, let's say you have someone separate patients into two groups, a target group and a control group. You then select a group of healers to remotely work on the target group, with the intention of healing them. They might use prayer, good thoughts, or whatever seems to work for them. The healers are not even informed who is in the group, nor are the patients told which group they are in. All the patients have essentially the same illnesses. At the end of a pre-determined study period, you have doctors who are blind to which people were in which group, independently judge how well the patients are doing. You end up with two lists of patients, those doing well and those who are not doing as well.

You are surprised to see that the ones who are doing really well are the ones listed as the target group. Have you just proven remote influencing? The answer is probably not. And the reason why is that the person who divided the patients into a target group and a control group at the outset of the experiment might have used precognition to make the selections.

An immediate argument would be something like,

"Okay, then let's run the experiment again, and this time we'll use a random number generator to determine which list the patients are put on." Now you have only to prove that generating random numbers are truly random, and that interaction with the machine is not really precognitive selection—deciding when to push the selection button to give you the number sequence you are looking for.

What to do?

What is interesting about this process is that it is entirely driven by a desire to prove remote influencing and not by a desire to heal more patients. In actuality, for some diseases there should be some statistical evidence that only a very small percentage of patients will ever get well or recover. These kinds of diseases should be the ones that are targeted while attempting to prove remote influencing. If you continually and statistically violate the bottom line expectation for getting well, then you are probably remote influencing, since even precognitive selection can't significantly bend that bottom line statistic for how many get well.

Many don't want to use terminal patients for a variety of reasons. There are ethical questions. What if you are successful with targeted patients and not the controls? Should you have told the controls they were controls? Have you restricted healing to a randomly selected few? There are even larger questions. For an illness that's near 100 percent terminal, would a 33 percent healing statistic open the door to science meddling in the miracle department? Arguments abound.

Why is all this important to remote viewing?

The importance lies within an automatic assumption that is made from the outset with remote viewing or psychic functioning, the belief that we in some way totally control what's actually happening. When the Remote Viewer is penetrating the target, whatever it might be, we assume that the Remote Viewer is totally in control. We also assume that the Remote Viewer, or psychic, is accessing information pertinent to the target. Many believe they are accessing this information from a general-reality records file, an Akashic one or otherwise. This implies both control and dipping into, listening to, tasting, or even stealing from this file. No one ever assumes that information is passed both ways, or that there is a sharing between the Remote Viewer, or psychic, and the actual target. But, if you look, I think there's plenty of evidence that this certainly might be happening with regard to humans.

Many of us have had the experience of suddenly knowing that one of our close family members is ill, or has had an accident. How did that happen? Were their first thoughts as the pain raced out through their body of us, the ones they care about? Was it fear of losing connection with us that made the sudden connection? We don't know. But, somehow it happened. We differentiate between sending and receiving information. Maybe that's not what's happening at all. Maybe when we tap into a target person, place, object, or thing, we actually share information with it. Maybe we view it as one way simply because cognition is taking place, we know when it's happening. Or in the case of objects or things, maybe just understanding the communication system would help. We probably don't understand that all trees communicate with each other, simply because we do not understand the language. So, we assume the communications is something we took, instead of shared.

I believe that when we perceive something—or target it, as in remote viewing—we are actually opening and sharing information. There is no actual broadcasting, transmission, or taking of the information. It is simply shared. This would certainly account for the observer effect noted in many areas of research. I see no radical difference between an observational effect resulting from physically watching something, and one accomplished through psychic observation.

Remote influencing is a significant issue that deserves a

lot of attention. Until proven otherwise, I would assume an exchange of information is taking place with a target long before I would assume I am simply taking information from it.

Manifestations and Apparitions

I bring this into a book concerned with the details surrounding remote viewing, for a couple of reasons. First, interactions with what appears to be conscious entities seem to be happening, or at least they are being reported, by psychics and people who are purportedly doing remote viewing. Secondly, based on personal experience they seem to be a natural byproduct of playing with remote viewing and the paranormal.

On occasion someone reports having interacted with a non-physical being or ephemeral conscious entity while attempting to do remote viewing. There are unsubstantiated reports of entities and discarnate beings interfering with the obtaining of information during remote viewing. I've had people tell me specifically that they were either directed or advised not to pursue certain targets by these entities. In rare cases, viewers report being assisted by such beings. Does this mean the entities are real and truly exist?

In spite of my own observations, I would have to say, your guess is as good as mine! I honestly do not know what to make of these events and have not yet reached any firm conclusions. I can only state what my own observations have been.

In most cases where I've had the experience, I have either been given information or have been made uncomfortable about pursuing it. By that I mean the experience has been either somewhat negative or somewhat positive.

I sense that where it was a positive event, I gladly accepted the information, which usually turned out to be about as good or bad as remote viewing information usually is. It certainly wasn't significantly better.

Where it turned into somewhat of a negative experience, I would not automatically attribute the negativity as an attempt to "warn me off," or to drive me away from the target. But, then, I've been doing this for twenty-one years, so I view these experiences more with curiosity than anything else. I try not to jump to conclusions, especially when there is insufficient data.

What actually may be going on is that I am in some way projecting a figure, or archetype from inside myself, which derives its origin from a positive or negative space that's in a more buried part of my unconscious. In other words, there is no clear or conscious connection between the information that I'm getting *vis-à-vis* a self-created entity, and that place inside me that already has a conviction or agreement with the information that's being presented. One could translate this to mean one of two things. I'm either giving myself information that I would ordinarily deny or reject, or I am going out of my way to fool myself.

After spending a considerable amount of time thinking about it, I would have to say that generally speaking, at least in my own experiences, these events, when they happen, have been about equally distributed between negative and positive. So, if I were forced to guess as to the reason for such experiences, it would be difficult to specify. My tentative feelings at the moment are that regardless of my negative or positive feelings for any specific experience, they are probably all rooted within some personal issue that touches on fear, at least to a sufficient degree that internally I am prevented from making a direct conscious-to-unconscious connection for data transfer. At the moment, however, this is only a guess.

So, are apparitions or communications with entities real? Yes, I would say so, at least to the extent that they have a profound effect on the one who experiences them.

Is the information received or provided accurate? Yes, at least to the degree that any other self-generated information can be; remote viewing, psychic, or otherwise. I would almost automatically assume that the messages are connected in some way with a deeper part of self, an archetype, or an area of the unconscious that is dealing with issues it cannot yet bring to the surface or is as yet unwilling to bring to the surface.

At this point, I'm not sure I would jump to any other conclusion about entities, regardless of how they might interact, appear, or identify themselves.

Appendix F

———————— ✸ ————————

List of Peer Review Journals

International Journal of Parpsychology
Parapsychology Foundation, Inc.
228 East 71st Street
New York, NY 10021

Journal of Scientific Exploration
Allen Marketing & Management
810 E. Tenth Street, P.O. Box 1897
Lawrence, KS 66044-8897

*The Journal of the American Society
for Psychical Research*
American Society for Psychical Research
5 West 73rd Street
New York, NY 10023

Journal of Parapsychology
Rhine Research Center
402 N. Buchanan Boulevard
Durham, NC 27701-1728

Suggested Zen Reading

Kapleau, Roshi Philip. 1989. *The Three Pillars of Zen: Teaching, Practice, and Enlightenment.* New York: Anchor Books.

Rosenberg, Larry. 1998. *Breath by Breath: The Liberating Practice of Insight Meditation.* Boston: Shambhala.

Suzuki, Daisetz Teitaro. 1987. *The Awakening of Zen.* Boston: Shambhala.

Suzuki, Shunryu. 1972. *Zen Mind, Beginner's Mind.* New York: Weatherhill.

Wangchen, Namgyal. 1995. *Awakening the Mind: Basic Buddhist Meditations.* Boston: Wisdom Publications.

About the Author

Joseph McMoneagle, STARGATE Remote Viewer #001, has gained a reputation as the discipline's foremost remote viewer since he began learning the way of RV'do in 1978. He has since provided support for a long list of government agencies and research institutes, and been awarded the Legion of Merit for "producing crucial and vital intelligence unavailable from any other source."

He is owner and director of Intuitive Intelligence Applications, Inc., and lives with his wife Nancy in the foothills of Virginia's Blue Ridge Mountains. *Remote Viewing Secrets* is his third book.

Index

A

B

Y

Yes/no questions. *See* Binary type questions

Z

Zen, 2-3, 179, 278

Hampton Roads Publishing Company

. . . for the evolving human spirit

Hampton Roads Publishing Company
publishes books on a variety of subjects including
metaphysics, health, complementary medicine,
visionary fiction, and other related topics.

For a copy of our latest catalog,
call toll-free, 800-766-8009,
or send your name and address to:

Hampton Roads Publishing Company, Inc.
1125 Stoney Ridge Road
Charlottesville, VA 22902
e-mail: hrpc@hrpub.com
www.hrpub.com